I am Chi Chi Iro, I own this story.

[5] God is in the midst of her; she shall not be moved: God shall help her, and that right early.

Psalm 46:5

THANK YOU NOTES

I want to first thank the Almighty, who makes all things beautiful in his time. I do not know what I have done to deserve such grace from God and I am grateful.

Tony Iro

I want to thank the love of my life, Tony Iro, who saw beauty and possibilities that no one could see at the time we met. Tony, you have encouraged me to go when I was the weakest. When I look in your eyes 24 years later, I see hope and a great future together. Your love gives me reason to soar.

My four princes

To my four princes, four times in a row you have proven me able in disabling circumstances. Thank you for being so understanding and caring. Thank you for never being embarrassed by my conditions. Thank you for seeing an able mother when you look at me.

Lady Beatrice Umeadi Anyaehie

To my late mother, Lady Beatrice Umeadi Anyaehie. Thank you for being that strength for me, I would never have accomplished the things that I have if you did not push me this hard. Thank you for sacrificing all to search for a better life for me.

My Dad

To my dad, late Chief Sir J.R. Anyaehie, thank you for being the supportive father that you were, through your hard work, I knew the advantage of not giving up in times of difficulties.

My Siblings

To my siblings, Dora, Ijeuru, Nnamdi, Ihuoma, Ndidi, Uncle Simon, Oby, and Lizzy—as well as their children, my numerous nephews and nieces. I want to thank you for all the kindness that you have shown me through the years.

My Late Mother in Law

To my late mother in law, Chief Mrs. Rose Candy Iromuanya. You took a risky decision by encouraging your young handsome son to put his future in the hands of a woman living with disabilities, thank you for believing in me.

Uncle Sam

To Uncle Sam, I would never have made it through the tough and difficult years without your acts of kindness. May the Lord reward you.

My Great Family and Friends

To my great family—the entire Anyaehie and Iromuanya clan—and friends, Olanma, Priscilla (hang in there, sis) Gina Ford, Olu, Conchita, Angela Patterson, Angela Morgan Ify, Udoamaka, Katrin, Onyinye, Chasidi, Tina, Sterling, and so many others too numerous to mention, I want to thank you for always seeing me as you did and allowing me to be all I wanted to be. To my good friends Alex Uzokwe and Chief Nnamdi Ekenna, thank you for encouraging me to write this book when I felt it was too hard to do.

To Ezioma and Myrtha thank you for being my midwives. To all my face book friends, I feel your love and I thank you for cheering me on. I love you all.

To the great women of Nkwerre that believed in me, Ijeoma Omekam, Aunty Ada, Ijeoma Chinaka, Mrs Evelyn Iheme, and Ngozi Agugua.

To my cerebral palsy advocates and groups all over, Femi Gbadebo, Dada, Chioma, Tina, Joy, Daniel—you make me keep going even when I am discouraged. To my other disability advocates, my good friends Ng, Tina, Tokunbor and Kasarachi, thank you for all you do for others.

To All Parents

To all parents of children living with disabilities, never lose hope.

CONTENTS

FOREWORD

"I am a survivor and I am not merely surviving, but thriving."

I have always known that what makes me appear strong to other people is the stories that I will not open up and air to allow healing to commence.

I bury memories from years past and find meaning in the present like there was no journey. On the contrary, the journey to become the Chi Chi Iro that you now know is one that has passed through so many difficult terrains, valleys, and mountains. It took all sorts of trials to become who I am now. According to Romans 5:3, "Tribulation worked patience."

I love to write, I painted a beautiful picture when I wrote in the past and felt comforted through that. Yet there was something missing in the stories I told. I needed to heal, I needed to forgive so that in telling these stories, I could find healing and peace, and maybe others can benefit from the stories and also heal.

One day my husband of twenty-four years, read one of my articles and said it was beautiful, but that I wrote like someone without a journey. I knew exactly what he meant. I knew he understood me and knew that there were parts of my experiences that were still raw. These experiences I chose not to share. I put some thought into what he said and prayed for the strength to do exactly what he suggested, and I am so glad I did. That is what gave me the inspiration for this book. By writing this book, I have travelled back almost fifty years, some stories made me marvel, some made me cry, others made me laugh so hard. What an incredible life I have been given the grace to live. These stories were told for several reasons. The first reason was for me, I needed to tell these stories to heal. I needed to understand why my mother was emotionless when I was growing up. I knew my mother did the things she did in my interest, but that knowledge did not heal the sadness in that little girl searching for answers.

The fact that my mother belonged to a generation that did not show emotions did not make it easy either. In my little mind, I was the cause of the sadness that I saw in her eyes. This book allowed me to choose how to tell the stories of all the experiences, good and bad, that I have gone through and helped me to laugh at the awkwardness, celebrate the victories, and accept the things I cannot change. The book brought me so much relief. I thank God that I decided to write it.

The second reason, I wrote this book was for my mother, I was so busy looking for my own answers that I never took a minute to understand my mother and the reasons she did things the way she did. As I started to write, I began to uncover the reasons for Mama's actions. I stepped into her shoes, most times as a mother, this helped me to understand what she went through. In doing this, I found the gift of forgiveness. I have one regret, and that is that when I got to this realization, Mama was gone. I wish she was here; I would have had a long healing talk with her. I know we would have ended that talk with some cleansing tears washing away all the pain and sorrow of years past. This is a tribute to Lady Beatrice Umeadi Anyaehie, the woman of strength, that sacrificed all so I can be. I salute you! You are my hero. All I am, I owe to you.

I wrote the book, to honor my Mother and other mothers of children living with disabilities. To you I say, may the Lord bless you for all you do. I know it cannot be easy worrying about a child that may not be able to give back to you in any way. As mothers you go on and on sacrificing in love because you have no choice.

I know sometimes you will feel that no one understands your pain. I hear you! I share that pain with you and I want to tell you to keep dreaming for your child. Push that child to be the best he or she can be, but please ask God to teach you balance. Push and then love. The love and affirmation goes a long way, tell your children how proud you are of their accomplishments.

The final group that I wrote for are all other people living with disabilities of any form, this includes those that have challenges that are not physical.

I believe that many people have limitations that are not physical, but because society does not put them in a box, we think they are coping, yet they cannot rise above their self-inflicted limitations. I want to let you know that all pain is the same, our stories may be different in detail, but I understand every frustration that you may be going through, especially for those living in Nigeria. I chose to make my experiences public so that you may have a role model and believe. know that all things are possible to those who believe (Matthew 9:23).

Growing up I had no role models, there was no one that looked like me that had accomplished the things that I aspired to, anyone living with disabilities in Nigeria at the time was hidden behind closed doors.

I am sitting here a few weeks from my fiftieth birthday, reflecting on this life that I have been given the chance to live, I find it very hard to believe because I did not think this was possible. It took a long time for this testimony to materialize, but I am extremely grateful to God. I feel and look amazing, I have seen worse days, but to him who can makes all things beautiful in his time, I give glory that I am fortunate to approach this milestone with a sound mind and body, surrounded by my husband and children, blessed with great family and friends, and a living testimony to the glory of God.

To God be the glory!

Everyone has a story and a journey,

telling a story is like healing a wound,

you have to air it to heal it.

If you cover it, it will delay the healing process.

You have to know the right time to tell a story.

You have to get to a destination to share your experiences.

You cannot stop to tell when in transition.

I just got to a rest stop, so I can share some.

My healing process has begun.

JOURNEY ON

It was April, 2011, my mother had been in the hospital for almost three months, my family hoped she would pull through. She had been in a hospital in Ghana under the supervision of an American based nurse who had been brought in to monitor her treatments. He was to get her stable  enough to be moved to a better hospital in the United Kingdom. God was faithful and kind, she was stable in a short time and flown to a hospital in London. We were hopeful, we felt she was in good hands.

There were good days and bad days, but we believed she would make it. One morning, my sister called me and told me her condition had deteriorated.

I have the facade of a very strong woman, because that was the way I was raised by the woman that I write about, but on the inside, I was the same as everybody else, a scared little girl; fragile and vulnerable. I would do anything to hide these feelings from others so they do not consider me frail and weak.

So, on that morning, looking to me for strength, one of my older sisters placed that call to me about my mother. In my usual way of dealing with stress, I immediately started shivering and making frequent trips to the bathroom, I have always dealt with stress that way since the day I sat for an external common entrance exam in my primary school at Aba. So back and forth, with my phone in my hands, I limped to the bathroom. My sister could not tell I was not doing well. She listened to the strength in my voice and she thought I could handle it.

On one of my trips to the bathroom, I fell. She could hear the racket on the other end and she asked if I was okay. I said yes. So many thoughts were racing through my mind. The first one was, maybe my mom would bounce back. In my practical way of dealing with things I wondered what I would do if she did not bounce back. This woman made me everything that I am today. I had not seen her much in recent months, but I knew the role she played in my life. Whatever I am today is a fulfillment of her dreams and her prayers. I tried to remain strong, I would never have imagined what emotions would go through my mind in the next hour. Then there was the issue of the guilt that I felt, maybe my presence would have made a difference. Why did I not make better effort to be by her side? Maybe my prayers would have kept her alive. I had prayed for others in the past and they were healed. My sister Ije's voice cut my thoughts short, she said she was going back to the hospital to check on Mama and that she would keep me posted. I was relieved to let her go. I needed to go to the Holy Spirit and crumble before him so he could build me up.

Once I got off the phone, I informed my husband of the details of my sister's call, we had just lost his mom three weeks prior, so he understood the emotions; we prayed and hoped for the best. I went before God just as I was, without my composure. I was shaking, shivering, and going back and forth to the bathroom, until slowly strength began to return.

Then the Lord spoke to me, "If this is the end, so what? She has lived a great life. It is time for both of you to journey on. She needs to continue her journey and you need to continue yours." I showered, dressed up, and waited. About thirty minutes later Ije arrived at Mama's hospital room, she called again and said, "I believe this is it." She had a dream about Mama some weeks earlier and it was exactly the sight she saw on getting to the hospital. My oldest sister took the phone and said, "Mama is going, say your goodbye. She can hear you, but she cannot speak back to you." I took a deep breath, I was no longer the last child of the woman on the other end of the phone, who was about to embark on a journey of no return. In the next few minutes I was going to take a journey myself. A journey to adulthood. One to complete independence, I was going to be motherless in the next few minutes.

A feeling of sadness, sorrow, grief and loneliness came over me, then I remembered I was a woman of God. Mama would need my strength at this time. She would have to release and travel light. I pulled myself together and I called out to her. "Mama! Nne m, several years ago, if you were faced with the possibility of this journey, I know exactly what would have been on your mind: 'God please spare my life, what will happen to Chinwe if I am not here?' But today, Mama, see what the Lord has done, see how far he has brought us." I continued with tears in my eyes, my voice cracking as I fought for the strength to get these words out because I knew we were on limited time. "Do not worry about me, I will be just fine. I implore you to let go and journey on. It has been a good life. God has been good to us." I could not say any more. I put the phone down and went quiet, seeking strength from God till the next call. By the time the next call came, I knew it was over.

My sister said, "She is gone."

I let out a scream, grief, sadness, and panic over took me. I went to the backyard and sat down. I cried and took in the event that had just happened. No one living could understand the trouble I was in. You see, she never said goodbye, she never told me she was proud of me, all this hard work that I had done and I really never heard, "You have done well," coming from her.

I felt that no one could understand my pain, my mom and I started this difficult journey together forty-four years earlier and now she was going to leave me without seeing all the dreams come true or all her prayers answered. MAMA! WHY?

Yet I kept still, hiding the tears I fought back and the tightness in my throat. She continued her journey and I continued mine, but in different realms.

The pain is still there, I have a lot of questions, I am still praying that one day I will get answers. My hope is that in telling this story, I can find some answers that will give me peace.

IN THE BEGINNING

There is a saying in my language that if you say yes, your God will say yes.

I said yes and as a result my God said yes to me.

From early childhood to date, forty-nine years and counting, it has been a revolving story of victory and triumph while overcoming great odds not just to survive but thrive.

My name is Chi Chi Iro, I am several things, but of everything that I am, none give me more pleasure than describing myself as a wife and mother of four sons. You may want to know why. The reason this gives me great pleasure is because, if you knew me you would know that this description of myself could only be true of someone like me in my dreams. It would be a mere impossibility if not for the grace of God and an unstoppable spirit for me to join the group of women from all over the world who answer to these two words: "Wife and Mother."

These words sound like music to my ears. I still pinch myself to make sure this is not a part of my never-ending dream life. I always say that I get the motivation to keep going from my dreams. Let me tell you how impossible this seemed for someone like me: I remember shortly after I gave birth to my first son, a lady that was related to me made a careless statement and said, "WOW! So when we count women that have children, we will count Chinwe as one?" Those words were hurtful, but they did not bother me, since God has just vindicated me. Sometimes you cannot help but thank God.

As humans, we think we have the power to dictate and decide who should be blessed a particular way. Thank God man is not God. God is so merciful and he always shows his great works in people that others will disqualify.

My favorite story to illustrate this, is the story of David in the Bible. 1 Samuel, Chapter 16. After the Lord had rejected Saul, he asked Samuel to go to the house of Jesse and that he had prepared himself a king, the Lord instructed him to also take his horn filled with oil and go. When Samuel got to the house of Jesse, he sanctified Jesse and his sons according to the Lord's bidding and the Bible says when Samuel saw Eliab, he said to himself, "surely this must be the Lord's anointed." But the Lord said to Samuel, "Do not look on his appearance or on the height of his stature, because I have rejected him. For the Lord sees not as man sees: man looks on the outward appearance, but the Lord looks on the heart." One by one Jesse made his sons pass by Samuel and the Lord rejected them and at this point Jesse was asked if he had another son? Listen to what Jesse said: "There remains yet the youngest, but behold, he is keeping the sheep." And Samuel said to Jesse, "Send and get him, for we will not sit down till he comes here." When David was fetched, the Lord asked Samuel to arise and anoint him for he is his choice and Samuel anointed him.

I just love this story in my language you can sum it up in a sentence. "Madụ abụ chị." Man can never be God. Imagine that even Jesse, the father of David, looked down on David due to his age. That is always what others do, they base your abilities on outside appearance and disqualify you. A common trend I see in people, when a person living with disabilities does something commendable, is the thinking that what the person with the disability has done is a surprise or a huge feat for someone with their limited abilities. It always makes me crack up laughing.

Every day people living with disabilities defy all odds, they say yes and God says yes to them. Thank God for social media! Daily, I lift my hands upwards in praise as I read stories of men and women defying great odds and doing wondrous things by the grace of God. On a personal note, I want to give all the glory to the Lord Almighty for saying yes to me and to the powers that be for conspiring to grant me the desires of my heart. What else can a girl wish for?

The purpose of my story is to let you know that you are unstoppable. You have the power to challenge any obstacles in your life as long as you are willing to put in the work it will take to  accomplish your dreams. My hope is that, in reading this book you will no longer see that which limits you, but that which enables you. Before you tell me that your case is different and that what limits you will be almost impossible to overcome, I invite you to sit back read, bring your faith with you and be encouraged. I hope I can succeed in making you a change your mind, so you can thrive.

3

ABOUT ME

I was born Chinwe Anyaehie, to Chief John Richard Anyaehie, a business man and philanthropist, and Beatrice Umeadi Anyaehie, in Nigeria in 1967. I was born during the Nigerian Biafran civil war. My mother, Da Beaty, Mama Ndidi or Aunty Beaty as she was fondly called by those that knew her, was a kind and soft spoken, beautiful woman. She was very wise. Before I was born, Da Beaty had had her fair share of pain and anguish in life. Apart from the fact that she was in a polygamous relationship, which was the style of most men of means in Nigeria at that time, she had a history of premature births, she had had over fifteen pregnancies before me and most of the babies, especially the boys, died.

At that time, it was said that baby girls had a higher success rate at thriving when born premature than the boys. Here she was, giving birth to another baby, this time thankfully a girl. While this was happening, there was a little problem. There was a war going on in Nigeria, most of the cities in the eastern parts of Nigeria that were under the Biafra control were destroyed. There was chaos everywhere.

Luckily, she was a patient in a famous hospital in Uyo that catholic missionaries had set up to offer better medical care to people in that region. By most standards she was in good hands, but in her mind as she was going into labor with me, she thought, not again! She was just entering the twenty-eighth week of her pregnancy and the chances of the baby surviving and thriving were very slim; however, she was a woman of great faith so despite the doubts she had in her mind, she decided to trust God.

A few weeks ago, I pulled up my medical records at my time of birth, I like to look at it because it makes me count my blessings. On the page my birth was recorded on, there were several other babies born at twenty-eight weeks, they all died. I was the only one born so early that was listed as alive, my condition was also listed as stable. That should tell you the fighting spirit I came into the world with.

Weighing in at a little under three pounds, with no incubators and very little medical care. The closet person that was in health care was my Aunty Titi (who is my greatest fan on facebook, presently she goes by Ugonma Grace). Mama took me home, keeping me warm with blankets and hot water bottles. From the account of my sister Ihuoma, who is now a Neonatal Intensive Care nurse, I caught every infection known to man, like a good fisherman catching his fish on his best day. In no time, with all the care I was receiving, I started to blossom. I looked like any other baby, very chubby and healthy. I met all my milestones until it was time to walk, at about nine months, Mama said she noticed I was walking on tip toes and that just did not look right to her. Since there was a war going on, traveling was limited. She started reaching out to nearby hospitals for answers, when that did not work, she resorted to local bone menders. I remember the bone menders, they had no time for mercy, they manipulated the bones to strengthen them. I remembered it was so painful. Initially I tried crying and screaming, but when that did not work. I just gave up and mastered how to keep the pain in. The pain management the local bone menders gave me has helped me in a lot of ways, today I can take any type of pain. I have a high tolerance for pain, sometimes it can be a negative trait because I may have a problem and not realize it because I ignore the pain.

Generally, it is a blessing, especially with labor and delivery, the four times I went through labor, I wondered why most women say it is painful.

The other thing I remember about the bone menders was the stench of the place. I was very young, but that smell has stuck with me. It was a combination of sweat and some massage oil, more like organic shea butter and some other oil that I cannot identify. I am sure they mixed their own medicine for potency.

I also remember one of the men, in a sleeveless t-shirt with skin that had been roasted by the harsh African sun. He always wore a raffia hat, but that did not help much in roasting of his skin. To this day, when I think of them I cringe. I hated that place and Mama took me there for my weekly sessions religiously.

Sometimes they would dig a hole and bury my legs in the sand. Initially I would cry out to Mama, hoping she would stop the session and take her little girl home, but no such luck. Apart from the few times she bothered to tell me it was for my own good, her face was emotionless. Completely blank! That look on Mama's face was puzzling to me at my tender age. I had known her to have a heart of gold. Over time, I realized the emotionless face was going to be Mama's default way of dealing with me.

Growing up I used to think to myself, surely she does not love me, but as I grew older and became the woman that I am now, I realized she loved me more than life itself.

Now that I am a mother and have my own children, I know how hard it must have been for her to put up that facade.

Do not ask me if the bone mending worked, I cannot answer that question, since I do not remember what my legs looked like before I started the process. The options were limited at that time and I know Mama would rather use them than leave me the way I was. One thing I know is that my doctors in the US several years later told me that my foot was completely broken and that it is nothing short of a miracle that I walk with the foot. My take is that as long as I can walk around unaided, whatever was done in the past must have helped.

As the months went by, and I started walking, it became obvious that my problems were more than walking on tip toe; I developed a very unusual gait. I was now walking with a conspicuous limp; it was also apparent I had weaknesses on the right side of my body. Mama's frown had deepened. She had a much bigger problem on her hands. You can understand why, this was happening at a time that disability in Nigeria was grossly misunderstood. It was thought that if you had a child with disabilities, it meant the gods were angry at you or that someone had put a curse on you. Again in the current structure of the marriage (which was polygamous) with children from three other mothers, she was the only one that had a child that was less than perfect. How little they knew, of course. Just like David, I was disqualified due to circumstances of my birth which I had no control of.

So Mama ran from pillar to post, seeking a solution. Her resolve to fix me grew as I blossomed into the prettiest little girl she ever saw.

Soon the war was over and Mama could travel far with me. She found the best hospital which was far away in Lagos. She would leave her other children in the care of her oldest daughter Dora and go with me for months. I wished I got first hand details from Mama about these trips to Igbobi Hospital in Lagos and if the trips helped.

Sometime in the early 70s, the trips to Lagos slowed down. I think I wiped away most of those memories. I do not remember much of the Lagos trips, but I definitely remember the bone menders which was long before Lagos. There must have been some trauma that erased my memories about Lagos.

As the Lagos trips slowed down, Mama became my trainer. I was now trying to do much more, I would notice her watch me pick things up or reach out to take things from her, I naturally used my left hand since it was stronger than the right. Mama would bark her orders, "YOUR RIGHT HAND, NOW!" I was always jumpy, which I later found to be a symptom of the condition I had, so when Mama barked, I jumped and obeyed. It did not take me long to know that if I did not want to jump at her voice, I had to try my best to do what she wanted, so I started willing the right hand to work like the left. Soon it was time to write. She would hand me the pen, which I had to receive with my right hand but I would plead with her, with tears running down my pretty face, that I could do better with my left, but she would ignore my pleas. In no time, I was attempting to scribble with my right hand, even though I held the pen as though I was going to strangle life out of it. Soon, I could write well with both hands even though my default hand was the left.

Mama would always say to me, 'your place is not with me, I do not want you stuck with me, you must have your own life, this is not a place for you.'

This was Mama's dream for me, she was saying those things in faith to me. At that time, the chances of any of these proclamation coming to pass was very, very slim almost impossible. But she continued to believe, she continued to push me to do more.

I remember one day, she called out to me and I went to her. She had a broom in front of her and she asked me to please sweep the room. This was a surprise to me as I came from a very privileged family and we had several domestic helpers. While I tried to process her instructions, she barked in the usual African mother tone, "MY FRIEND, SWEEP THAT FLOOR." I jumped and started sweeping with my left hand, she barked again, "WHAT ARE YOU DOING?" I quickly switched hands and she said, "Good girl." To this day, whenever I pick up a broom, I look back to see if Mama is there.

Soon it was time for elementary school, I remember going to a school near my home, the children teased me frequently and I would go home and tell Mama that I did not want to go back to the school the next day. She let me believe she was going to grant me those wishes and let me stay home, but the next morning, she would ask the helps to get me ready for school. I was always in shock, since she seemed to have agreed with me the night before. After breakfast she would tell me it was time to go to school.

I would object, crying and she would get out her big cane. She walked behind me, threatening to use the cane, till we got to school; if I fell she picked me up and we continued. Soon I knew she had no tolerance for my antics.

Eating was another issue, I was a very picky eater, swallowing a mouth full of anything made me want to gag, I believe this was due to weak throat muscles. Yam and beans were my least favorites. I just hated eating. Mama would give instructions to have rice cooked and once it was ready she would pour beans in the rice. My heart broke in pieces as I wondered why she was so mean. If I turned 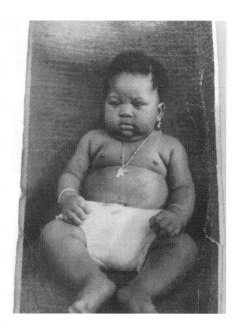 down whatever was served to me, she made me go hungry. Soon I made an effort to attempt to eat every type of food or run the risk of starvation. Mama was tough!

"Delight thyself also in the LORD; and he shall give thee the desires of thine heart."

(Psalm 37:4)

4

A MOTHER'S PRAYER

*L*ike I said earlier, Mama's prayer for me was for independence; she wanted me to have my own life. She knew this was not going to be easy to accomplish since people living with disability were locked up and they depended on their families for everything. It would be considered a waste of resources to invest in anyone living with any form of disability. There were no role models; no one with my type of disabilities had done the things Mama wanted for me, she saw potentials that I did not see in myself at that time. One by one, I started meeting and exceeding most of her expectations. The more I accomplished, the more goals she set. She did not expect any less from me.

She started handing me tools that would help in the journey ahead, she was a devout Christian, she started early to teach me the word of God and how to live an upright life. From an early age, she noticed that I was an empty vessel, she could fill me up. I was the youngest child and she deposited everything that she did not have the chance to teach my older siblings.

She thought me how to knit and crochet as well as several other skills.

The most valuable of the things she taught were her words of wisdom. They were proverbs from my local dialect in Igbo. If you are familiar with the famous Things Fall Apart then you will know that proverbs are the oil that the Igbos use to eat their words. These words combined with Christian teachings help me through any difficult situations daily.

She always used the phrase "Anya wụ onye ụjọ" meaning 'the eyes are cowards.' What this means is that if you are not brave, your eyes will scope a task and send the message of fear to the brain and you will be overwhelmed by what you are seeing, but if you prepare yourself and brave it and tackle one thing at a time then you will be amazed at what you can accomplish. This has been the most valuable of all my lessons. Whenever I am faced with a difficult task, I do some self-talk and say this to myself, then I start with one little area and before you know it, I will see the light at the end of the tunnel. I bring this mindset to everything I do in life. If I decide to clean and go upstairs to the boy's rooms, I scope the place as I wonder if I missed the tornado warning the night before, instantly I say "Anya wụ onye ụjọ" to myself and take a trash bag, pick a spot in the room, and start separating the trash from the treasure, in no time, I will make such huge progress. That will amaze anyone, simply because I believed it was a possibility. Daily, I use these skills, no matter the circumstances, it could be cleaning, like I mentioned earlier, cooking, or even writing a book; whatever it is that you think is too big to tackle, you can do it. It is true that my children are growing up in a different culture, I try to repeat some of these phrases to them and then translate. I know someday these phrases may come handy to one of them.

One lesson in particular still cracks me up, because as much as Mama tried, she did not make much progress on this one. She taught me always to tell the truth and there were times I told the truth, but in doing that it created a problem and she would discipline me. I would cry out, "But Mama it is the truth and you have always told me to uphold the truth." One day she had a talk with me after one of my truth telling episodes, she said with that distant wise woman look in her eyes "Nwa m', ọwụ gị ezi okwu n'ile anya hụrụ ka ọnụ n'ekwu." My child, it is not all truth that the eyes see that the mouth speaks. Now this one threw me off completely since at that time I did not understand it, I wondered if she no longer wanted me to uphold the truth. Several years later, I hear Mama loud and clear, "Some people have been murdered for telling the truth, families have been divided because someone was bold enough to tell the truth but no one actually benefited from telling an unnecessary truth."

To date, I still battle with this particular one, sometimes it takes wisdom to know when to speak and when to hold your peace. To drive this point home, we can refer to the Bible in 1 Corinthians 6:12 "Everything is permissible for me, but not all things are beneficial. Everything is permissible for me."

I can go on and on with the life skills I inherited from my wise Mum that influence my actions today, she taught me to prioritize and focus on what is important. She would always tell me, "Onye ụlọ ya na agba ọkụ a na gịachụ oke." When your house is burning, looking for the rat that has been terrorizing you and your family is unwise. What this means is that if you have your priorities right, you can take care of the important things and then go back and take care of the smaller things.

Her favorite saying of all times was an English one, "Know thy self is not a curse." This is basically about your identity—knowing who you are and your peculiar circumstance.

5

MIRROR MIRROR ON THE WALL

After the war, we moved to a new city, it was a more sophisticated city than the one we had lived in. I guess Mama decided to settle things in her life a bit, so the medical treatments sort of slowed down; however, due to the training I had at home, I continued to get stronger.

I was more aware of my surroundings now and it was clear to me that I was different, not because I felt different, I was used to the way I walked. In the past, people's gait looked slightly different from mine. It did not take me too long to figure out that I was not just a little different, but very different.

Some of my brothers lived about a mile away, we would go down the road to visit them or play with friends that lived close to them. Once we hit the streets, total strangers would stop just to stare at me in that typical African fashion, they would act like they were so touched by my predicament. They would cry out, "My goodness! This very beautiful girl, why did this happen to you? Who did this to you? The devil is so wicked o!" As soon as they started, I would just freeze. Then I would gather enough strength to rebut whatever they were saying to me by pointing out their flaws and rolling my big round eyes. I hated it, I would just say, "look at you, you yourself are not perfect, why are you talking about me, when you have things wrong with you?" I am sure they thought I was ungrateful, but I was not, I just needed to block out the negative and unpleasant words they were saying to me. I often wonder what it is about people living with cerebral palsy that draws so much attention from strangers. I have thought long about this and it is fascinating. Think about it, you may see someone in a wheelchair and it seems normal, you may see someone with a walker or someone that just had a stroke and it may seem normal too. Once someone with cerebral palsy shows up in the mall...Tada! All hell will break loose, adults open their mouths and stare from the corners of their eyes, while the children stare and ask their parents to explain the meaning of what they are seeing. I have a ready answer that makes me feel better so that these stares do not make me feel like a freak of nature.

This is my answer: It is because we, living with cerebral palsy, try so hard to challenge the tightness of our muscles, we feel very thankful that we can move, we challenge the non-conforming parts of our bodies with all our strength and keep going. Each step, each action takes everything we have to achieve, yet we strive. That is why we are resilient and unstoppable.

Every time I had one of the negative encounters on the streets of Aba, I would come home sad, then a few minutes later, I would go in front of the mirror and repeat the good part of what they said to me which was that I was very pretty to myself. Once my thoughts were directed at my positives, I would get a really warm feeling, all the sadness would disappear.

I would look at my face, my hair, and my skinny body and I would say, 'not bad at all.' One remarkable thing is that once my eyes went to look below my waist, I would will myself to stop.

I never looked at the image of my legs in the mirror. What this did for me, was that it gave me the benefit of living my life like any other person. I also avoided seeing my legs in my shadow. I was going in for reconstructive surgery two years ago, I believed my leg would be very close to perfect after the surgery. With that hope, my husband and I recorded a video just before they wheeled me away into the theatre. When I saw the video, I could not believe my eyes, each step was this jerking movement, I clutched at everything in sight to stabilize myself. I asked my husband Tony if my legs were that bad and he was puzzled that I was not aware how bad they were. I opened my mind to look at the legs on that one occasion because I felt change was coming real soon. I thought the surgery would make me close to perfect. I do not know if it did or not since I really do not see my legs. Sometimes denial is good, it makes you accomplish what is in front of you without the inhibitions of the true state of things. Daily, I would stand in front of the mirror and take in all the goodness that I was seeing, admitting that it was good and quickly ignoring my legs. The thought of my legs would make me sigh at times, but only for a second. Then I would go back to the things that made me happy. Soon I was fully aware of who I was. My beauty and personality blew even me away, most times until someone else reminded me of the leg by saying, "Such beauty! Why did this have to happen?"

Though my self-confidence was great, there was still this wish to be like other children. I really could not say why I had that desire, since things were going quite well for me. Looking back, I think my reasons were mostly cosmetic. I had a great family, I was smart and beautiful, I had no difficulty doing the things I desired since my disability was no longer an inconvenience but a nuisance, yet day by day, I wished I could get a miracle.

"I will praise thee; for I am fearfully and wonderfully made: marvelous are thy works; and that my soul knoweth right well."

(Psalm 139:14)

6

LET SOMEBODY SHOUT ALLELUIA!

One day, I was having one of those 'why me' moments and these moments made me sit alone, wishing and dreaming things could be different. This period was the peak of the Pentecostal movement in Nigeria. I sat in our family room in Aba and I was partially watching the TV and feeling sorry for myself when a commercial came on the television. It was a commercial about an American evangelist visiting my city for a crusade, the voice of the man on the commercial bellowed, "The blind will see, the deaf will hear, and the lame will walk." I glanced at my leg and sadly admitted I belonged to the last group; the lame. Then my big eyes just brightened with the thought that maybe this was what I was hoping for all my life, my chance had come to be like every other girl, so I went in search of Mama, praying she would find a way for me to meet this evangelist that could fix my leg.

I found Mama downstairs and asked her if she could come with me. I said there was this man on TV that said he could fix my leg, I was surprised she did not argue with me, she just followed me. During that time, it was a no no for a child to give orders to a parent, but she quietly followed me, maybe she desired this miracle as much as I did.

We got to the living room, I can still remember this living room, it had black and white terrazzo floors and the furniture was royal blue, I remember the big wood veneer box that housed the television. By the time we got to the living room, the commercial was over, I told her they would run it again. We both sat there waiting for the commercial to come back on, each harboring thoughts of how our lives were about to change. I was thinking that if this worked, I would be perfect, I could do ballet dancing, I could do more shakara; I could not contain my excitement. On Mama's end, I am sure she was praying this could be the answer to her prayers. Her pretty little girl could just be made whole. Her prayers were about to be answered, this would mean a break for her, she could focus on her life as well as her other children, the world would know that she served a living God. We sat silently waiting for the commercial, each too afraid to voice what they were thinking. I nervously played with my hair. Finally, the commercial came back on and I asked her, "Can we please go?" She smiled and answered, "Of course." That was a beautiful smile, it was a smile of one, hopeful for greater things. I did not remember Mama smiling that way at me any time in the past.

I found it hard to contain my joy in the days before the crusade, all I could think of was how many things would change for me in a few days and how I would live my life with ease. No more stares! Yes!

My heart was pounding, I was too excited, my life was about to change. Finally, the day came and I was dressed up in one of my pretty dresses, my thick black hair put in a bun with a ribbon. I had on my white socks with frills and black Mary Janes, they were the only type of shoes I could wear because they had straps to hold my feet down. We arrived at the stadium and it was packed with people. There were parents with children living with disabilities, men and women hoping for an encounter with the Lord, there was so much excitement in the air. The evangelist and his interpreter said repeatedly, "Your visit today will not be in vain, the Lord is going to change your life, everything that held you down will be loosened today, if you believe it shout a thunderous alleluia!" We all responded to him, some were clapping, some singing, others praying. I had a million thoughts running through my mind. I hoped they would call me out with over five thousand people in the stadium. "I hope my healing happens today." The man of God continued with his preaching. He took his sermon from Mark 2 verses 1-2 and taught on the paralyzed man that was brought by his friends, hoping that Jesus would heal him, but on getting to Jesus his friends realized that the crowd was great, they decided to let him down through the roof. He explained that when Jesus saw the effort that the friends went through, he was touched. He forgave the man his sins and healed him. He said this will be the story of most of you here.

As if the Lord heard me, the evangelist paused and became very quiet, like he was receiving a message from God then he spoke with this clear loud voice. "There is a little girl standing at this part of the stadium (He pointed in my direction) she has something wrong with her legs, bring her up!"

"Mama he is calling us," I chanted, my heart was pounding. Mama lifted me in her arms as she made her way through the crowd and within seconds she had us standing before the man of God on the podium, now Mama was the one showing her excitement. She was wringing her hands and waving them repeatedly and as he commenced his prayers, she started weeping and saying, "Amen! Amen!" Soon he was done praying and he asked me to walk up and down the platform. I did my best walk and the crowd erupted. They were screaming. I felt like a superstar on the runway. Then he ended by saying my healing would be permanent in Jesus name. At this time Mama was crying uncontrollably and saying, "Thank you, Jesus" over and over. My joy knew no bounds, I was healed. I was now like every other girl in the world, was I not?

Not only did he say I was healed, he said it was permanent, meaning it would no longer be my story.

Day by day, I rejoiced at my fortune and replaced my "Why me" with "God has remembered me." I changed the way I did everything. I was different or was I?

Remember, I was not quite aware of my disability, I did not know how bad it looked to others and even when they tried to tell me, I shut them out. Now they would not have any reasons to see any imperfection, I thought. Anytime I was alone, I would do my version of catwalks before the mirror and smile to myself. I would climb to a high spot and jump with no inhibitions and clap, as if I could not do that before. Somehow nobody stopped me on the streets or stared at me the months after the healing so it helped to confirm to me that healing was done and final. Every now and again, I would nurse a little doubt and I would ask my family, "My leg is good now right?" They would look at me and answer a weak yes. I so much wanted to believe that yes and I did. This proves what we believe is what we will experience. I believed I was healed.

I continued to float around enjoying my perceived fortune, until one day I had a fight with one of my brothers, Emeka, he wanted to say something to me that would help him get back at me. He was so angry that he said, "I do not know what is wrong with you. You remember, all the times you asked me if your leg was healed and I said yes to you? I lied, your leg is still very, very bad. I thought he was just being mean, I held him on his shoulders and pleaded with him to tell me he was joking. I had tears in my eyes as he confirmed to me that he was serious and he meant every word, my heart stopped beating. I reluctantly dropped my hands to my sides. To say I was devastated would be an understatement. As quickly as my hopes were raised on the day of the crusade, my life came crashing down, there were several questions floating around in my brain and I did not have answers to them. Did the evangelist lie? Does God lie? What was it the people at the crusade saw that made them clap? Was I healed and then unhealed? But he said it was permanent. How do I start living my life as a person living with disabilities again?

"I am as a wonder unto many; but thou art my strong refuge." (Psalm 71:7)

7

THE REVELATION

The Biafran war had long ended, the Igbos were very wounded and in recovery. They had lost all their possessions, to escape the pogrom in other parts of the country. Most of them abandoned what they had acquired over a life time, a lot of Igbos that were born in other parts of Nigeria now had to return to their homeland where they were merely strangers. Even though the  government had announced a no victor, no vanquished policy. The action on ground was different.

All Igbo bank account holders, no matter how much they owned were left with just twenty pounds. Their jobs had been taken away from them and filled by others.

Even closer to home, the government announced the most disenfranchising thing of all by enacting the abandoned property edict which said, in essence, that all the properties that were acquired by Igbo men and women, that they abandoned to run to safety during the war, were deemed abandoned. Overnight, All Igbo men and women were dispossessed of the houses they had worked hard to build and total strangers became the owners of their houses. The Igbos were a broken lot, there was so much rebuilding to do.

John Richard Anyaehie was one of those men that was rebuilding with a lot of pain, even though he ran to safety in his village Nkwerre. He had abandoned his livelihood in Port Harcourt, he had lost all his savings, but as is common with the Igbo people they had to look forward. He had made a few connections during the war that allowed him to make some money to relocate his family to another city with promises.

He was not going to invest anywhere outside the Igbo land. Going forward, so that he would not have a repeat of what happened to Igbos in the Biafran war.

Aba was safer ground and he had built a state of the art home for the family, it had all the luxuries a home could boast of in the early 70s, including a swimming pool.

Daddy. unlike my Mum. had younger children that could call him Daddy since that was what was fashionable at their schools; I had the luxury of calling him that too. At home he was called Oga Sir behind his back, he was not a very tall man, but he was revered. He loved to dress up and was very charismatic.

He had a penchant for discovering great business opportunities and because of this gift, it did not take him a long time to bounce right back after the war.

Daddy had children from four women, even though all the children were technically raised by my mother.

He travelled all the time due to business demands, everyone was afraid of Oga Sir; when he honked at the gates, everyone at home straightened up. I was one child that did not really fear him. He could not believe how bold I was. Whenever he did something I did not agree with I challenged him, this was new to him as everyone around him did what he wanted. Later I found out that he actually admired my boldness. One of the incidents that confirmed this to me was after I gave birth to my first child, we had told one of his friends who was very proud of us to go tell Daddy that we had just had a baby. His friend, Uncle Theo, travelled to the village over the weekend and said to him in Igbo, "Chinwe amuọla." Chinwe has given birth to a baby. In Igbo if you do not listen carefully it could sound like, "Chinwe anwụọla." Chinwe is dead. So he screamed and asked, "What happened?" Uncle Theo answered, "NO! She just had a baby!" and my dad was happy, shocked and surprised. He said, "Just like that?" Then he said, "Elelịa nwa ite y'agbọ nyụọ ọkụ." You cannot ignore a boiling pot because of the size, it will surprise you by boiling over. He was basically saying, do not underestimate any one, they may just surprise you. I was not surprised he made that comment. I had heard him say to others in the past that I was very tough and he wished the boys in the family were like me.

Now, business was beginning to bounce back from the devastation of the war, the first daughter of the family, Dorothy, had just finished her secondary school education. Daddy decided to send her to London to study the ways of the white man, while she was in school, she studied the way things were done in the western world and relayed information back to him. It was on one of these fact finding missions that she explored medical treatments for me in London.

Since he was doing very well back home—having just secured a franchise with Toyota, he had several income yielding properties all over Nigeria, and with the help of my older sister, he had bought his first property in London—arranging medical treatment for me in London was not much of a problem.

So in 1978, myself and my sister, Uchenna, were shipped off to London with our big sister who we called Sister Dora. Uchenna was to keep me company, while I went through medical treatment. It was on this trip that I was diagnosed as having cerebral palsy officially, the first suggestion the doctors had was for consistent physical therapy, so daily we went to a center that was filled with children with all types of disabilities and had physical therapy sessions.

It was at this center that I remember having direct encounter with other children living with disabilities since I never met them in Nigeria; most of them had conditions that were worse than mine. I wrote in my first book about the one occasion I chatted with a boy in a wheel chair and I could not understand why he was strapped to his chair. I said to him, "If I were you, I would just get up and walk." He was quite witty and he took one look at me and said, "If I were you, I would walk with my leg straight."

Through the years, I have grown to understand the concept of limitations and how much desires and dreams can help overcome limits.

London was a totally new world for Uchenna and I; it was lonely, cold and boring. We missed home. When we were not at the therapy center, we were at home dancing or watching TV.

Other times we just giggled like silly little girls. We found reasons to laugh at everyone and everything. Soon the time came for us to return back home to Aba. I do not really know if that first trip to London made any difference to my legs, no one commented on improvements and after my huge disappointment following the crusade, I had learnt my lesson and I was not going to ask anyone. So I kept going, I focused on doing the best I could with what I had.

Getting back to Nigeria, it was time to get back on track with my education. I had been granted admission into a unity school, Federal Government Girls' College, Owerri. The unity schools in Nigeria were created by the federal government to unite children from different tribes and backgrounds. They were great schools, I was excited to be admitted into a federal school because they were highly competitive, but there was one problem, there was no federal school in Aba where we lived. The closest school was in Owerri which was hours away. I had to live at the school.

Fear replaced my excitement. How would I leave home? That meant I would be with other girls. What if they did not accept me? How would I cope?

As usual, Mama had no doubts in her mind that I was going to boarding school. She started preparing me to leave home. I was petrified. Eventually the day came, she asked me to get ready to go and my things were packed up in the car. I kept hoping she would change her mind and ask the driver to turn around and go back home.

The ride was very quiet. We were both scared, but we could not acknowledge that to one another. I had tears in my eyes but Mama was the last person you wanted to see your tears. Also I was afraid she was crying too and if she saw my tears then she would break down. We got to the school, she gave me a piece of advice. "You are here as an ambassador of the family, do not bring shame to the family." Then she finished off with her proverbial "A word is enough for the wise." Mama spoke very few words at times like these. She met briefly with the principal and my house mistress, handed me over to the house mistress, turned around, and left. Looking back now, I know she must have cried on her way home, she must have been as scared as I was.

Settling down in Federal Owerri, as we called my school, was unnerving. First they had to find a bed where I could sleep on the bottom bunk since it will not be logical for me to climb to the top bunk, another reminder that I was different. I was taking it all in, calculating where and how I could plug myself in.

One day, I saw some of my classmates playing and I wanted to join them, a particular girl who later became my friend told me she would love for me to join them, but she did not want me to fall, because if I fell, then my dad would put them all in jail. I do not think she said it to hurt me, she was just concerned. That statement hit me hard. I went back to my hostel and laid down on my bed. Then I remembered an exercise I used to do when I was home. This was not my regular day dreaming. It was my 'why me' exercise, with tears running down my face, I started asking God why

I was different. I also asked why he lied to me after the crusade and I got an answer that shocked me. "It is true that the healing you received that day was not physical, however, you received healing that will enable you to do whatever you want to do. I will give you the grace. Do you know that if you can do anything that they can do and do it better they will accept you?" I said to myself 'that is going to be very hard, they will not even give me a chance to try.' And the voice said, "Keep trying, they will eventually let you." It was hard, I did not want to be rejected, so I kept to myself the rest of the term.

Soon it was time to go home. I took my report card home not knowing the contents because it was addressed to my dad. He opened the report card and sent for me. He asked me why one of my teachers made a comment that I was anti-social? I said I did not know, he took off his glasses and told me that he hoped for my sake, I was not being arrogant. I answered no sir, he warned me that if he received this kind of report again, I would be in big trouble.

I can do all things through Christ which strengtheneth me.

(Phillipians 4:13)

FINDING ME

I will always be grateful for Federal Owerri and for how it helped me find myself. I returned to school the next term with Daddy's threat and a determination to be accepted. All these things were going on in the mind of an eleven-year-old. The routine at school was tough, we had to walk to the cafeteria every morning, eat breakfast then go to class. After school there was lunch, then siesta, and prep—which is study hall—then back again to the hostel, looking back now I do not know how I coped, but I did, mostly all that was expected of me. Apart from the times I excused myself from manual labor, I never sought to be excluded from anything. I asked to be excused from manual labor because I did not want to cut grass, not because I could not do it, but because I did not like it. Bit by bit the girls started trusting my strength.

When I noticed it was working, I continued by doing more. I would seek out things that the tough girls did and do them so I would be called tough too; if you did not know you would think I was being rebellious.

Every morning the girls were to leave the hostel at a particular time and head to the cafeteria, once the time came, they would lock the hostel doors. If you did not leave on time, you would be locked in and punished afterwards. I noticed the tough girls ignored the matron's call to get out on time and then jumped out of the window afterwards, but God help you if the matron caught you jumping out, then you will be taken to the principal for greater punishment.

I found window jumping to be a very fascinating adventure. I joined the tough girls. I was caught a few times and taken to the principal. Each time I would say, "With all due respect, Ma, do I look like I could jump this high window with my legs?" She would take one look at my legs and agree with me that it was impossible for one with my physical limitations to jump such a high window. It happened this way so many times that the matron would start doubting what she saw.

Gradually, I gained confidence as well as notoriety from my actions, it was music to my ears. I was discovering the powers I had and my ability to use the disability card to my advantage. I was being accepted into the world of the able and it did not cost too much to do that.

I would not be the person that I am today without Federal Owerri. Boarding school equipped me with the skills I needed. Yes, Mama made me do chores at home, but at school I was responsible for my life. I tried very hard to cope and in no time, I blended quite well with the other girls. We had inspection on Saturday mornings, during inspections our bed making skills were graded as well as the organization of our lockers. You could get plus or minus marks for performance. If I had wanted special treatment or exemptions from most of the tasks I could have gotten that, but that was not an option I desired to take. I wanted to be like the other girls, not different.

After the initial hesitation of accepting me, they allowed me to be who I wanted to be. By showing the girls I was capable, they were fine with my being one of them.

I remember a fashion show we had, we were asked to bring our best clothes to model and the organizers suggested I give my clothes to someone else for fear that I might trip while modeling. I told them if I did not wear my clothes, nobody would wear them. Well they just asked me to do whatever I wanted to do. I guess they thought they had given me fair warning and I refused to heed. Looking back, I recollect I was so afraid, I was asking myself why I had opened my big mouth to say I could model. Now I had to prove myself and God help me if anything went wrong, they would not give me the chance again.

It was too late to change my mind, I stood in the line waiting to be called. Some girls were called before me, then it was my turn. My heart was pounding, I felt like turning back but of course, I had worked too hard for this acceptance. I took a deep breath and then tuned to denial mode, in my mind I was the best model ever, soon I heard clapping and cheering and then it was over.

I got an award that night, my close friends told me I did an awesome job, only God knows what they saw. For me, I could not believe I did it.

I was still trembling from the thought of what would have happened if I missed my steps.

That night, as the other girls slept during lights out, I replayed the day's events over and over in my mind. Thanking God for sparing me yet again and before I finally dozed off to sleep, I remember saying to myself, "Chinwe, note to self, learn how to shut up in the future, you were just lucky you did not fall." I knew somehow I was not going to keep to that counsel though. I enjoyed the attention. The adrenaline rush was awesome. I always remember that day at the school cafeteria when I have to do something and I am nervous.

I remind myself that the worst thing that could happened was that I would not have done as well as I anticipated, but I may get rewarded for participation. In life, there is no reward for lack of participation, but there is always recognition for participation. Nothing illustrates this as much as kindergarten graduation ceremony. I often wondered why schools waste time celebrating kindergarteners, but as I think deeply, I appreciate this more and more. If you have had a child participate in one of these ceremonies, you hide your frustration when you see what they get awards for.

Award for funniest student, teacher's helper, most improved award. It is like the teachers spend time and come up with the reason to celebrate every child just because they were part of the team. There is a life lesson here; in showing up you contribute to the team. Another example is in a sports team, once the team wins, everyone gets a trophy, even the worst players receive a trophy under the cover of the best players.

By the time I got to the last year in Federal Owerri, I had acquired skills to survive and thrive in every aspect of life, I owe much gratitude to every little girl that accepted and included me in their lives. You helped in giving me the confidence I have today.

The lesson I appreciate the most, is that if you want other people to open their arms and include you, you have to be willing to open your arms and embrace others. I would not have had success at the school, if I had remained an introvert. The girls would let me be and feel sorry for me. We were very young and a lot of them had never been in close proximity to a person living with disability, but they did a fantastic job. I made it easy for them to do this by showing them I was capable.

No one owes us the duty of making us feel accepted. People have their lives to live. You are the only one that can discover yourself and project your discovery to others so they can relate to you.

Embracing your uniqueness is a personal journey. Not just for people living with disability but for everyone. I found myself, my strengths, my weaknesses, and my voice in this school. Sometimes I had to be disobedient to get the recognition I sought, just in a childish harmless way, like bringing more than the allowed amount of personal clothes or wearing my personal clothes on school days. I was lucky this was never reported to my parents, they would have dealt with me mercilessly. The school and the girls were exactly what I needed to discover myself. It was an enabling environment and I emerged after five years knowing fully who I had grown to become. I was amused at the way I was viewed by several of my schoolmates, some saw a rebel, some saw the girl that lit up a room, others saw a spoiled child, and a few saw me for who I truly was. I did not mind any of these opinions, they were all great as long as no one saw me as a person with disabilities that could not do anything. I was only seeking inclusion and it did not matter what I had to do to achieve that. Mission accomplished!

8

MY REINTRODUCTION

My mother had done a great job laying the wonderful foundation and Federal Owerri gave me the skills to survive and thrive. The next stage of life was now for me to practice everything that had been deposited into me. The mirror was still a huge part of my life, I was now very lean and tall—extremely leggy. The funny thing though, was in the real sense I was not counted as one of the hotties in Federal Owerri. The girls had little cliques, they had their own definition of who they recognized as beautiful, these beauties—according to them—had great body shapes or 'figure eight' as we used to call it, or great legs.

I do not think I was identified with any of these groups, but that did not deter me. I had my mirror, so after I graduated high school I reinvented the power of my mirror. I liked what it showed me. Not bad at all.

Soon I mastered my body and my assets. I was beautiful and I knew it! I was mysterious and had a great personality about me, I was soon becoming familiar with make-up. I took great care picking out my clothes and dressing up. I was quickly becoming a woman and even though I was afraid of this next stage, I knew the only way, I could conquer the fear was to be uniquely me.

I recollect that every morning, I got up early and dolled up, a habit I still practice today, the difference is that I no longer care for a lot of makeup.

There was this time the family was spending summer in London; that was the routine for every summer vacation. The London vacations were the only times we dined with Daddy. So this morning, everyone came down to the table and I was the only one missing, then Daddy asked, "Where is Chinwe?" Then he said in Igbo "O ga ejikeme jikeme." She is dolling herself up. Everyone burst out laughing. I was coming to the dining room and I heard that, I really did not find it funny, but now when I remember it I laugh. I think I used all that effort in my appearance to take attention from my legs and it worked.

Boy was I pretty. I was still very naive though, even in the summer before going college.

As I matured, I knew I had to take time and master most of the things that adults did if I was going to venture into this territory with the least negative attention. I put a lot of thought into everything that I did, I spent time accepting and embracing that I was different, but in spite of this I was someone worthy of being desired.

The stares in the street continued, but they were the usual ones mixed with those that were attracted to this beautiful young lady. I loved every bit of the attention, I took all of it in and used them to build my self-esteem.

Sometimes the admiration was not immediate because they were not sure to what extent I could relate. I was still very much a loner and introverted, these attributes gave me the ability to withdraw from the crowd occasionally and think deeply about how I was going to approach the next stage.

It was at this time that I came to the realization that there was still a lot of ignorance surrounding disability. Not everyone who was drawn to my beauty when they saw me sitting would stick around when I stood up. Even though this made me sad initially, I quickly rebutted that thought with the fact that I was beautiful, kind, thoughtful, smart, and I would be an asset to anyone willing to be my friend. Then I would quickly say to myself, "It will be their loss, they will lose the chance to know an amazing woman."

This is a skill that I use in ministering to people with low self-esteem. There are a lot of people that do not have any form of disability. They look great, but believe no one will want them. I let them know they are amazing and if someone does not want to be friends with them that will be the other person's loss.

Because my self-esteem had improved greatly, I started enjoying the shock on people's faces when they found out about my legs.

I remember once, I had spent summer holidays in London with the family and I still had some treatments to get done, so the rest of the family went back home. When it was time to return home, I dressed up real nice and boarded the plane for Port Harcourt from Heathrow airport; I knew I was looking very nice. The plane was not quite full, halfway through the trip, this guy asked me if he could sit next to me (He probably did not see me limping in). With all the makeup I was wearing, I guess he thought I was older. We started chatting and he said he liked me a lot and asked if I had a boyfriend; I said no. As he was getting deeper into the conversation, I had this mischievous look on my face, it was time to find out if he would stay longer or flee, so I stopped him and told him I needed to go to the bathroom. He stood up to let me get by. I made the walk to the bathroom, I could tell he was looking at me from the back. I spent a little time in the bathroom to make it look authentic and then returned. He was still there, but he was very quiet. He did not mutter a word after that and he had been extremely talkative before then. I just smiled and brought out my book and started reading. He did not even have the guts to ask me why I walked differently. I bet he was upset with himself for not knowing there was something wrong. Thank God I knew my worth or that particular encounter would have set me back.

Summer was over and it was time for college. My campus was in Aba, the same city where I lived; initially I went from home then I moved into the hostel. It was an open hall and we had corners, in no time I figured I could enclose my corner to be a room.

There was so much action happening on campus. There were parties every night and, like I said earlier, I enjoyed partying and dancing. I really did not want to go into the dating scene yet, I was very afraid of that and just not ready to deal with it.

I had some great friends and life was good. Because of the experience I had in boarding school, adjusting was not much of a problem. The only difference with Federal Owerri was that in college I was responsible for myself, there were no bells to remind me that it was time for lectures or time to eat. In fact, I could decide not to attend lectures or eat. I could leave campus when I chose. There were no parents, matrons, or teachers telling me what to do. There was absolute liberty. Some girls were from different backgrounds. Some were naive and sheltered like me, others were mature and experienced in life matters, and some were even married.

One day I went out with one of my friends, she was one of the experienced ones, as we walked leisurely she said, "can I ask you a question?" She asked if I had ever had a boyfriend. I said no, she told me never to admit that to anyone or they would think I was a baby. As you know, I did not want to appear different from other girls, so I made a mental note to get a boyfriend. How I was going to do that, I had no clue. One thing I knew was that it was not going to be easy. The way the first boyfriend came was quite unexpected.

There was this girl, she was about two years my senior in school, and one day we got chatting, as we talked I could tell she really liked me and before we parted ways that day we had become friends. Later she would come frequently to visit me in my cubicle. She told me that she would like to introduce her boyfriend to me, she said she knew he would really like me. So one day she brought him over, she was right, we became friends instantly. She kept telling him she was right in believing he would like me. Anyway, as the weeks went by her boyfriend started visiting me alone. Initially, this was puzzling to me, but we enjoyed each other's company and to me it was a harmless friendship. One day he shocked me by asking if he could date me, I asked him why since he was already in a relationship with my friend. He said he liked me too and we agreed we would be good friends, but with no strings attached.

Daily he would come to visit, then someone told this girl that her boyfriend was spending a lot of time with me. One day this girl and her friend stopped me and told me that I should stay away from this guy and that I should know the guy would not want anything to do with me because of my crocked leg. This hurt me really bad, especially since I was respecting her feelings by just being friends with her guy. I did not mean any harm, but it was one of those things you had to endure when you are a person living with disability. Other women disqualified you when it came to men.

One day, I got my lucky break. In those days the hostels had communal bathrooms, it was typical for girls to shower in open stalls with no doors, so I was passing by one of the bathrooms in this girl's hostel. She was in the process of taking a shower and when she saw me, she immediately bent over. I had heard that she had oversized breasts for her tiny body, but I did not know how big they were; they were humongous! So as she bent over, I moved closer and I said to her, "I did not know you had anything about your body that you were not proud of." I thought she was perfect. When I said this, she just kept quiet and did not look up. I also told her that after that day, I did not expect her to talk about me again. She was in shock as I left her and walked away. From that day forward we had a silent understanding.

The incident with this girl taught me a huge lesson. It taught me that no one was perfect. Some imperfections could be handled by taking action. This girl could buy a good bra or she could just accept her body. On the other hand, physical disability cannot be hidden. Knowing that no one was perfect gave me this comfort to keep going.

I kept going, doing my best not to feel different and trying to blend, it was getting easier by the day. After the incidence with that girl with huge parts, I found peace in knowing that even your worst critic has flaws.

I stopped worrying about what other people thought about me, knowing that if I dug deeper in the lives of the people that appeared perfect, I would find something they wished was different.

Most of the burden of being different at this point had disappeared. It was now a question of what I wanted to do and if I was prepared to put in the effort I needed to accomplish that.

9

TAKING CONTROL

*I*n life, we have full control of our actions and reactions. You cannot continue to blame others for things that they did or did not do. You have the power! My experiences in college taught me fully how to take control of circumstances no matter how negative they may appear. I have two illustrations on how you can change circumstances. The first one, is a beauty queen in a pageant, her name has just been announced and she nervously takes that walk out. As she walks, the heel on her six-inch stiletto shoes breaks. She slips and falls. She has two choices and she has to make her decisions swiftly. She could focus on how she has reduced her chances of winning and start to cry, the organizers will rush to her, they will be empathetic, they may even send an emergency crew that may take her in a stretcher and wheel her away; but that will not guarantee her a winning slot. On the other hand, if she thought, "You know what, this is a setback, I can really bounce back and finish my routine and see how that goes," then she may just accomplish something. You never know how far you can get if you try. That's the way it is in life. Every setback presents an opportunity for the diligent to press on. Even for the very spiritual amongst us, no matter how much you pray, if you do not back your prayers by action or inaction, you will not get the desired results. God is not emotional, your prayers and your "why me" thoughts will not produce results without the relevant actions. Trials will surely come but even apostle Paul said it in Philippians 3:14, "I press on toward the goal to win the prize for which God has called me heavenward in Christ Jesus."

You have to press on no matter what.

For me, I really do not have a choice, it is either I press on or I let go of my dreams and then what will be my purpose?

Everyone has a right to their opinions. People living with disabilities feel offended when others do not relate with them the way they expect. Classifying other people is natural, we all do it one way or the other. We are reacting to what we do not know. We are usually unsure of associating with what is "alien" to us, so we react with fear and when we are afraid we freeze and become uncomfortable. Most people will not bother dealing with anything they do not understand. There is no need to let that bother you. As long as they keep it modest and to themselves you just go ahead and make your own rules.

We start at an early stage in life to decide what we like and what we do not like, most of the classifications at this age of innocence are not based on anything concrete like race, color, abilities, or status. It is just a mere exercise of one's choice. That is why in kindergarten a child will be drawn to another because of their pigtails or the cartoon character on their lunch box. They are innocently exercising their free will.

Later in life, in middle or high school, it becomes what sports you play, what you wear, who you attract, or what car you drive. This gets more complicated as we form cliques and exclude others based on how they look and what they own. It continues through all the stages of adult life.

Have you ever watched a kindergarten group at a playground? There is always a leader playing with a bunch of other kids and one lonely child sitting on his own. Is there a problem with playing on your own? No, but in most cases, you can tell there is a problem; the lonely child keeps looking over his shoulder at the group with a sad look on his face.

The more he looks over at them the less they want him in their group, he is indirectly telling them that he feels inferior to them and that their acceptance of him matters. He is giving them the power instead of taking control and setting up his own domain. What do you think would happen if this child was accustomed to playing by himself and setting up his own stage? What would happen is that whenever the group looked his way, he would seem to be having so much fun! Eventually one by one the kids from the group would start slowly coming over to him and before you know it he would be leading his own pack.

An incident in college taught me this valuable lesson. It was common in my days for college students to travel out of station to party. This one time I left my university to go to University of Nigeria Nsukka, which was a few hours away, to attend a party. We got there a few hours early. As usual, I took great care dressing up, I knew I looked very pretty. I went to the party in the company of some of my friends. All the girls were on one side of the room, giggling and talking excitedly while secretly admiring the men on the opposite side of the room.

As the music started, the finest guy in the group (and I guess the boldest) took steps toward the opposite side of the room, checking the girls out. I would be flattered if he was coming toward me, but I did not want us to be on the dance floor alone while everyone stared at us. As he got closer to me, my heart was pounding and I was saying a prayer hoping he would not pick me. I guess the guy was attracted to the pretty face, in no time he was standing in front of me asking if he could dance with me. Oh no! I thought, as he took my hand and started heading toward the dance floor. Remember this was not my school, here they did not know much about me. Suddenly, he realized something was wrong and he did not know what to do, at least he was gracious enough not to overreact. He gently leaned over and in a very sexy baritone voice asked me if he should take me back to my seat. I was kind of expecting that reaction, but I was not going to let him make me the talk of the day. I leaned in and said in my sexiest voice, "You know, if I could not dance, I would not come with you. Do you want to give it a try?" I could not predict the answer, but I prayed he would give me the chance to prove myself. He paused for a minute, still holding my hand, then he headed toward the dance floor. That day I danced like my life depended on it. I could not tell if my heart was pounding from being so close to this hunk or the fact that if I made any mistakes I would ruin my life and people would gather around me with pity in their eyes and then this young man would feel so bad for giving me a chance. I quickly brought back my focus as Lionel Ritchie's "All Night Long" boomed from the loudspeakers.

We danced to several other songs. Occasionally my knight in shining armor would lean in again and ask if I was tired and I would say no. From time to time, other guys would come and ask him if they could have me for a minute and he would say no, that I was his for the whole night.

Finally, the tempo of the music changed, it switched from very fast music to something slower. He pulled me closer as the song went on, I closed my eyes and moved closer while trying very hard not to be too close. I let my mind drift to how great the night turned out to be because I made a decision to give life a chance not knowing what it would bring, like that beauty queen that stood up and took a chance, I took a chance and it worked out for me.

The next time he asked if I was tired, I said yes and he gently walked me back to my seat. WOW! I had just rewritten a negative event by making it something memorable.

What a wonderful evening! I was ready to go home.

Before I left the party, I noticed an older guy looking at me, I was wondering why. It was not unusual for guys that were not students to be at such parties. He finally made his way to me and asked if he could have a word with me and I said yes. He told me he was amazed at my personality, he had a daughter born with disabilities and he wanted to know what he could do to make her grow up just like me. I told him to do just one thing, let her be herself. He looked at me with tears in his eyes and I left the party that night with so much fulfillment.

I often wondered how that night would have turned out if I had agreed to him walking me back to my seat at the beginning of the dance. Knowing the way Nigerians react to people living with disabilities, they would smother me with pity and some would say, "Poor girl! Eeyah! Why did she come to the party with her bad legs?"

Instead, on my own, I took control; I defined me by my terms! On our way home, I kept hearing "All Night Long" over and over in my head. This lesson has had one of the greatest impacts on who I became.

From time to time there would be a situation like the one I narrated above, but the outcome of this particular incident always made me press on.

Every day is a chance to let someone else know "I am aware you may not understand me, but if you can give me a chance, I will show you that I can be fun, that I am like everybody else." I approach it with a clear mind not to get offended. If you let things like that bother you, you will end up being bitter and angry. You have the power to control what happens to you.

I want to mention that accepting the effect you have on others and controlling how that bothers you will get better with time, the more you successfully do things the more you will build your strength with your successes, while knowing where your limits lie. It is true that we use the cliché "no limits" all the time to reflect strength, but another one of Mama's lessons comes in handy here. "Know thy self." True, take on things that challenge you, but please do not embark on journeys that you know you have no abilities to do. Only take on risks that you know you are equipped to perform to some extent. For instance, I had danced several times in the past. I knew that was a task I could easily handle even though the fact that I was at an unfamiliar location made this situation more awkward. I knew if I kept calm, I would do it sufficiently. Was my intention to be the best dancer on the floor? Oh no! I was going to be doing my best considering my tight muscles, but guess what? Most dancing partners go in search of okay dancers with attitude and ability. Attitude I had! Oh yes! I was a sight for sore eyes, sometimes some sets of eyes do not believe what they are seeing when they look at me. I challenge what they know as normal. They feel like saying, 'How dare you come to our world? Do you not know you are disabled?' I was daring, I was a lot of fun.

Very soon college was conquered. Sadly it was time to venture into another new territory. One very far from home. Little did I know that this next journey would change everything. Nigerian Law School, Lagos! Here I come!

10

CHANCE OF A LIFETIME

*E*very graduate of law, on successfully completing a four-year college training, attends the Nigerian Law School, before sitting for the bar exams. Upon passing the bar exams they would meet the requirements of the Nigerian Bar Association to be called to bar.

In 1988, there was one central law school, unlike now. Now the law school has been decentralized.

At the law school, there were both foreign-trained and home-trained law graduates.

Most students with parents living outside of Lagos could live in the hostel during the one-year training. For some reason, I could not get into the hostel immediately, they told me most of the open slots for accommodation had been filled. Thinking back, I could have used my disability card, using it would have worked wonders, but that was not who I was. I was not here to get pity and be treated differently, I was there to be like everybody else.

So I let my parents know I was having problems finding somewhere close to school to live. They took a few days and came back to me, they had found a family that they trusted that I could stay with. They gave me the address and I went to visit.

It was the family of my Aunty Ethel. God bless her soul. Aunty Ethel was an older lawyer, she was beautiful and smart, no wonder my parents picked her out of all the people they knew. She was fun and easy going. She had three children at that time, a set of twin girls and a boy, soon we found out she was expecting a fourth. Her younger sister Angela was also attending law school with me. Aunty was an excellent host, she became my second mummy, years after law school, whenever she was visiting my parents they would tell me Second Mummy came to visit. She followed up on my progress until she went to be with the Lord a few years ago.

Most of the best memories from law school were the ones from Aunty Ethel's home.

She lived at a high rise called "One Thousand and Four."

It was for federal civil servants, the only negative thing I remember from her building was the fact that the elevators hardly worked so I always had to climb up and down several flights of stairs, this was not just a few steps. Looking back, I think that was how I developed my love for climbing stairs.

Soon the law school hostel got in touch with me, the space was now available for me. With mixed feelings, I bid my favorite aunt and her family goodbye and moved on.

The hostel was filled with beautiful young women, some went to school with me, others grew up in Aba, and quite a number of them were people that I did not know. I was glad to have my good friend Conchy, she had been my friend from our first year in college. Initially we had not been friends, but once we became friends, we became very close. Conchy was an extremely loyal friend who thought the world of me. However, Conchy also wanted to tell good looking men she met about me. You will see where that got me soon. Another great friend was Fatima Usman, popularly called Asampete. Her close friends called her Asa. She was beautiful with the darkest skin and the whitest teeth ever. Asa was a popular and funny one. I first heard her name on the loudspeakers as I came to live in the hostel, every thirty minutes an announcement will come on: "Ms. Fatima Usman, visitor for you." I kept wondering who this was until I met her.

Asa, my dear friend, was loyal to the core. Whenever she was close to my village, she would go visit Mama's grave and take flowers. She went to school at Onitsha, even though she was Hausa, she could speak a little Igbo. Asa was always there for me, she lived with me after law school; she was a member of my family. She always called me "Nne."

I was in Nigeria in 2013 to visit my dad, Asa heard I was in town and showed up at the gates in my village, she spent time with me there and then followed me back to Lagos. I really wanted to go home, I had overstayed and Tony was complaining. I was hoping the airline would let me get on the next flight, but on getting to the airport, we realized the planes were packed full. Asa asked me to sit in one spot while she paced up and down the airport looking for help. Finally, she returned and said, "Nne, you are getting on the plane. I spoke to the manager and they have a spot for you." That was my Asa. She would do anything for me. You can imagine my shock one day when I logged on to Facebook and someone had written that she died the day before. I was heartbroken, to this day I mourn my friend.

Back to law school...daily we were taken by bus to the campus, the auditorium was large in capacity. There were young graduates everywhere with black and white suits and their leather briefcases milling on the multi-level floor, the lectures were very serious business. Conchy and I wanted to take our lectures seriously, but we also wanted to have a little bit of fun while doing so. So we found permanent seats toward the back, where the notorious back-benchers sat, away from the prying eyes of the lecturers.

One day, Conchy nudged me in the arm and pointed at another back bencher, this time a guy; I looked at him and I shook my head in rejection and she asked me why. I told her that would be cradle robbing as I really was not into the habit of dating very young guys. But with her eyes twinkling with excitement she said, "Chisco, he is so cute, I think he will like you." Really that guy was extremely young, he looked like a little boy, he was cute alright, but seriously there was no attraction. Little did I know that in the months to come this young man would be part of my story.

The guy liked to dress up. He was good looking, truth be told, and he had very broad shoulders. I knew nothing about him and I was not going to waste my time finding out. Every day as he walked into class, Conchy would say hi to him and then ask me if I would not reconsider my earlier decisions not to flirt with him and I would tell her no.

One day, I came to class and I misplaced my identity card and as I looked around, there was a card with the name Chinwe on it and without thinking I reached out for it. But that guy told me it was his card. I asked if his name was Chinwe and he said yes. I thought he was joking but he was very serious. I took a look at the card and I saw that it said 'Anthony Chinwe Iromuanya.' That blew my mind completely as I had never seen a guy go by that name till that day. That day started the first day of a long friendship. We started talking just a bit more. He was kind of reserved at the time, I knew how to get people like him to open up, with no pressure, in very short time. I rolled my big black eyes at him and he started talking. I no longer got upset when Conchy pointed him out, in fact, I was starting to consider robbing that cradle. I also found out that Tony was not as young as he looked, he had very boyish look that he has maintained. We were actually the same age, at least that was a plus. Soon he was talking, he told me he was the second of three children, his father died when he was three years old and they were raised by their mom. He was mourning his best friend that just died in a car crash. Daily we talked and he was a great listener, always smiling. I was getting quite fond of him, but I had to keep my cool. I was not ready to get into any messy relationship.

I was not really dating anyone at that time, I had been in a couple of relationships, some were really great guys, but I did not think any of them had what I was looking for. Deep inside me, I knew what I was looking for, I did not know if it was possible, but I had been praying about it.

I knew some of the people I dated in the past liked me a lot, but I also knew it would take a truly matured mind to want something permanent with me. It wasn't because I was not wife material, it was just because they were not ready to live with the burden of marrying someone like me. At this time, I was twenty-one. I had figured life out and I was truthful about my unique situation. Somehow at this time, I had had enough of being in relationships that did not amount to much.

I was not very religious at the time but because of Mama, I knew how to talk to God. I had gone to God in all honesty and prayed. "Dear God, give me a man that will love me as I am and I will be loyal to him till you call me home." I was not born again when I said this prayer, but I knew I was going to honor this promise. I was just tired of not considered good enough

The months rolled by, soon it was February and Valentine's Day was fast approaching, the girls in the hostel had planned a little game. We were going to send cards to any guys that another girl was fantasizing over. It was going to be anonymous. One of the girls, Chijioke, gave the card to Tony and instead of taking it and playing along, he wanted to know who the admirer was. I had made Chijioke promise not to tell, but Tony was not going to take no for an answer. He persisted till she told him, I do not know if he suspected at that time that I was the one, I also did not know if he was attracted to me before then, but I know one thing for sure after that Valentine's Day incident, the friendship moved to a whole new level. One thing was different about Iro (as his friends from college called him) he had no problem introducing me to anybody as his friend. Soon we were always together and I met his friends. Initially they did not mind seeing us together, but as we got closer, I could tell a lot of them really did not approve.

One day as we were sitting in class, one of the girls that came from the same village with me came to my seat and told me that she heard my brother-in-law had just died, I asked her how she knew. She told me that she just found out from someone who just returned from the village.

Communications were not as easy in 1988, there were no cell phones. I fell apart and Tony was by my side to comfort me as I cried. I told him my sister was too young to be a widow and that she had two children under the age of two; he reminded me that his own Mom was much younger when his dad died but she still coped. I could not keep my tears back. My brother-in-law was very kind to me. He was a good man. The news of his death came just as we were about the start our exams. I knew concentrating on my studies was going to be a problem. Tony offered to study with me.

Funny how in life there are no straight stories, events both happy and sad, all propel you closer to God's plans for you. From these very sad times, new opportunities were opening. We studied very hard, and when we were not practicing, we got up to the usual mischief that young people got up to.

We were just two young people having fun.

In my private moments, I would say to myself, "I just like the way this guy makes me feel. There was something he understood about being in a relationship with someone like me that none of the others understood." Then I would rein my thoughts in. "Calm down, Chinwe...do not let your imagination run wild, just enjoy the ride." One day he had a visitor at the

law school. It was an older lady, she was very beautiful; the two appeared extremely close and he called her Lolo. I kept to myself as they carried on with their conversations. I was just a little bit jealous but I knew it will be out of place to expect too much from him, we were just good friends. It would be inappropriate to expect much from him. So I pretended everything was okay.

When the lady was about to leave, he brought her to me and said, "I want to introduce you to someone. Meet my mum." I was speechless, I looked from Tony to his mom and wondered what type of people they were. Did they have a patent to youth? She smiled and asked how I was? I said a weak "fine." I apologized for not knowing she was his mother, if I knew I would have been more receptive.

She told me she was accustomed to the shock on girls' faces whenever she was introduced as his mom. As he left to see her off, I tried to analyze what I just witnessed. Such beautiful and decent people I thought, but as usual I pulled my thoughts in.

Soon law school was over. It was time to go back home. How was I supposed to leave these memories behind and carry on? I really do not know the answer, but as with most things in life you learn to cope. Tony and I talked often on the phone. I tried to keep my mind busy by pretending to be okay, there was also the occasional worry about the result of the bar exams. Sometimes I got worried that we may have been too distracted to study adequately. I prayed for both of us to pass because if either one of us failed we would blame the other. Luckily, very early on a December morning, the results were released in the National Newspapers, we both passed. THANK GOD!

For the 'call to bar' ceremony, I was back in Lagos and that was another great chance to see him.

11

NEW VISTAS

*O*nce you get 'called to bar' the next logical thing was to sign up for the National Youth Service; in Nigeria every graduate had to serve the country for one year. Tony had told me he was posted to Port Harcourt—Another of those plans that was divinely orchestrated. Port Harcourt was barely an hour from my home. I was posted to Cross River State initially, I knew it would be perfect to be in the same place with Tony, so I pulled some strings and I was granted the request. I was overjoyed. Now it was time to plan for an apartment. I told Daddy I needed an apartment in Port Harcourt since he owned several properties there. He let out a loud laugh as if he was asking 'Who exactly will be living in this apartment all alone?' I downplayed my frustration, it was obvious he was not familiar with my strengths, anyway time would tell.

He told me he had one apartment that the tenants had not paid rent for a long time, he said if I could get the tenants out, I could have the apartment.

Knowing Dad, he used that to test me. He had used several lawyers in the past to try to retrieve the property and they were unsuccessful. The tenant was a teacher at a school

Port Harcourt was notorious for not honoring their obligations, but I knew just the right arguments to use. Daddy could have given me any other apartment, but he also wanted to make it a little tough on me. He was also carrying out his usual "show me venture." See, Daddy was a successful business man that believed that you cannot want something without putting in some hard work to get it. He had a lot of liquidity and would finance any project, if and only if the person proposing the project has already initiated the venture. Whenever someone brought a proposal he would tell them to show him venture, usually most people took this challenge as a rejection. For me I saw the apartment issue as yet another challenge.

Armed with the powers from Daddy, I travelled to Port Harcourt, and camped in my sister Lizzy's apartment, which was in the same complex but on the lower floor. Lizzy was the same sister whose husband passed while I was in law school. The morning after my arrival, I went upstairs and knocked on the door of the apartment that would hopefully soon be mine. The lady living there was Stella. I introduced myself and instantly she became hostile. I informed her of my mission, not minding the hostility. I let her know I was just putting her on notice that I was going to legally inform her employers of my intention to evict her. While I was talking to her, I could see the inside of the apartment through the open door, it was huge, but it was a mess. My heart sank and I wondered if I had not bitten more than I could chew this time, but it was too late to turn back. I went back downstairs to my sister's apartment, I got a piece of paper and started constructing my letter, I did not really know what impact my letter would have, but it was a good place to start.

I started by introducing the property and mentioning my relationship to my father. I explained that I had recently been posted to Port Harcourt and I was in need of a place to reside. I explained that it was within my rights to retrieve the property based on these needs. I also said I was aware they had not paid rent for several years. I found the address of the school, had the letter delivered to the school, and started the waiting game.

Much to my surprise, a week later, I got my response back. I was overjoyed. They apologized for the non-payment and said they had given the staff one month to vacate. WOW! Amazing news, I did not tell my dad right away, I was going to wait for the lady to leave before I told him. Some days later, Ms. Stella was putting her pots and pans and few pieces of furniture together, within two weeks she had moved. Good news traveled fast, my reputation as a no-nonsense girl spread within and outside the family. Several people thought I was mean, but I did not owe them any apologies. Finally, I made that trip to my father. I took the key to the apartment and the letter from the school. I told him I had the apartment back. In his usual way he concealed his admiration, but I could tell he was very proud of me. Mama told me that he said I had done on my own what several lawyers could not manage.

No one knew why I wanted my own apartment as I had a boyfriend in the same city. I came from a very strict Igbo family; you did not bring a man home unless you were married to him. Tunes were changing. I had graduated from law school at a very young age, I was working, and if I lived on my own, I could have a guy visit without my parent's knowledge.

Tony had already moved to Port Harcourt, he was staying with some friends of his family. He had been deployed to the Nigerian Port Authority for his national service.

I told him about the apartment. He came to visit and we went upstairs to see it. This time I had full access. I had the chance to look through and take an inventory of what needed to be done. The place was worse than the first time; there was trash and debris everywhere, there were no cabinets in the kitchen, and there was only one bathroom with a stained tub.

I was discouraged. Tony in his usual way, made me feel better by telling me he had seen worse. He assured me that with a little bit of TLC we could make the place look like paradise. I trusted him and I was not a quitter. We spent some time talking about all the things we could do, we played a bit, after that he went home while I went back to my sister's. Now I had the apartment, but what next? I had nothing, not even a bed and it was going to be lonely being up there by myself when Tony was not there. In my usual self-talk I said, "Be careful what you wish for."

Reluctantly, I started to put my things together. I just had my personal belongings. I moved my things upstairs and started my own life with nothing in my apartment. I got help and cleaned the apartment out. It was looking better now that all the things had been moved out. Over that weekend, Mama came to visit, she brought me a huge mattress, it was from a mattress company that my dad owned. Mama also brought this sweet little girl, her name was Mercy. Mercy's sister Grace had lived with Mama for years and their mother was one of Mama's very few friends.

Mama told me to treat Mercy as my daughter, she told me to enroll her in school as soon as I could. She did not waste too much time with her usual advice. She spent about an hour, left Mercy with me and said goodbye. Thinking back, I think she also brought a broom. I was not just gaining my independence. I had now gone from a twenty-one-year-old youngster to being responsible for another individual.

Now that I had a brand new mattress and a clean house with permanent company, it suddenly felt like home.

I was deployed to a bank for my National Service it was called Continent Merchant Bank, they were partners with Chase Manhattan Bank in the United States—there was a banking boom at that time in Nigeria and the banking industry was the place to be. Apart from working in an extremely luxurious environment, the attraction for me was that they, paid the Youth Corpers—as we were called then—additional allowance; it was good money for a young girl. I also started selling goods on the side, as well as making furniture.

In the weeks that followed, I enrolled Mercy in school. In the morning when I headed to work, she went to school, by the time I returned home, she was back from school and had the entire place spic and span. Most evenings after work, Tony would come over. Whenever he was around we would plan out the work we were going to do in the apartment. There was this uneven arch in the apartment, we sought an idea that would make it look much better, we thought burnt bricks would look really great, so we went in search of burnt bricks and finally our friend George Jumbo told us that his uncle sold them. They worked out so well, covering the unevenness in the arch.

It was a brilliant idea, once completed we had leftover bricks which we used to build something similar to a fireplace, but without the heat; we put in an air conditioner in that spot. There was a huge back wall and it was the first thing that you saw when you opened the front door. We found an artist who designed a mural and drew a design on the wall. Then we elevated that back wall and placed a beautiful dining set on the elevation. It was amazing! Well planned and executed.

Life was good, things were coming together.

It would not be completely true to say that the relationship between Tony and I was perfect; we had our issues, we argued frequently, if there was anything that we did not agree on we argued. There were no pretenses, I was stubborn and opinionated and I wanted to stay that way; he hated to lose an argument and he had met his match. Making up after an argument was also easy for us. Even though I had wanted a more mature guy, Tony was wise beyond his years, but he had playful childlike behavior at times. What Tony lacked in maturity he made up for with his heart, he had a compassionate heart. He also spoiled me with great gifts, it was not just the quality of his gifts it was how he gave them.

I will never forget the next time Valentine's Day came around. This time I worked at the bank the entire day and when it was time to go home, I went downstairs to my car. I remember that car, it was a brand new Honda Civic, it was grey. One of my bank customers had been involved in a Ponzi scheme, things went wrong and he wanted to sell off his assets, he had bought the car a month prior and he paid a fortune. He wanted to sell it at a fraction of the cost, I told him I knew someone that may buy it. Daddy never missed a good deal, so I arranged to visit him on my day off. I had called earlier to let Dad know I was bringing someone over. He told me he would be in his guest house in Oteri. When we got there, after the introductions, we went straight to the point regarding the car.

He agreed it was a great deal, he asked the guy for his title, looked at it, wrote him a check, then the man handed him the keys. He turned around and gave me the keys. He told me the car was for me. Looking back, it was in appreciation for the venture I showed him earlier. Remember when I got the apartment back for him?

Back to my story about the Valentine's Day celebrations. I got to the car and the driver was nowhere to be seen, that was unusual, since he knew what time I got off. I pulled at the door hoping it was open and maybe he made a quick trip to the restroom, the door was locked. That was when my eyes caught the most beautiful sight a woman could behold on any Valentine's Day. There were beautifully wrapped presents and cards all over the seats, I was so excited and could not wait to see what this was all about. I called out to my friends to come see what I was looking at. We always showed off such emotional gestures. Soon the driver emerged with Tony. To finish off the evening, we went to my favorite restaurant for dinner.

As I opened the presents I was doing a mental check and wondering how I could match this. I had not really spent much thought on presents for Valentine's Day, but I did not want him to think I didn't care. Anyway I had a nice white shirt in my sales inventory, I could give that to him. That would really not be a good match, but it would work for now. I could also add payment in kind.

Looking through the presents, I could not help wondering how much money and planning went into that day. He bought a ninety-piece dinner set, there were flowers and a beautiful blue and white paisley scarf that I still have. There were several cards, on them he addressed me as "baby" and signed as "me," then he had drawn the picture of a palm tree with birds on it. This has always been his signature for love.

Tony is a born romantic! I think after some time he kind of eased off on some of the details because I was the exact opposite. I think I was guarded in my emotions because I did not want it to look like I was forcing anyone to date me. As different as we both are, there is one thing you can tell about us, we truly love each other.

When we were not acting like two teenagers, we were arguing, we could hardly agree on anything. Our friends were kind of worried, they felt lawyers should not date lawyers. They said there was too much legalese going on. Most of his friends liked the idea of having a girl they could have a conversation with, but also wanted that sort of lordship that existed with most transitional African marriages. Anyway we were not talking marriage here, we were just having a great time; or were we not?

Truth be told, the idea of marriage was not something that I entertained at this time. Apart from the fact that we were still very young, there was the issue of building our careers. On my end, it would have been unfair to saddle this wonderful young man with the difficult burden of marrying me, not because I was not beautiful and thoughtful, but because things were just not that easy. The beautiful soul that Tony was, he was always introducing me to people as his girlfriend, I noticed how people looked at him with pity. I just felt he was deluded, I felt he did not know what he was getting himself into. Tony just kept going, he was unstoppable in his love. He was not treating me like he did because of marriage, he was treating me that way because he saw me as human. Being married to him for close to twenty-four years, I always say our relationship has never been the conventional African relationship.

Anyway let me close out on the early Port Harcourt days. There are too many stories waiting to be told.

12

PUTTING MY CARDS ON THE TABLE

After Tony went back to Lagos, we kept in touch. We were speaking daily on the phone. I missed him a lot and I really do not do well with long distance relationships, but life had to go on. Sometimes I would go to Lagos and spend time with him, his mom was more liberal so staying in his place when I was in Lagos was not a problem. By this time most of his family and friends knew who I was. Sometimes out of concern they would tell him to find a way to get out of the relationship before it was too late, others would ask his mom why she was letting her son date a disabled(which is what they called me). Tony did not entertain anyone talking to him about me, he was already sold. On his mom's part she would ask the people that worried about my relationship with her son, "If she was your daughter would you not want someone to marry her?" Seriously, marriage to Tony or any Nigerian at this point was far from my mind. Even though he fit 'the man of my dreams' and was now that man.

I was willing to give that dream up as I got older. Some of the reasons I had was that I did not want anyone to marry me out of pity. Secondly, I did not want to deal with watching the person I love carry the burden of being with me. Thirdly, the pressure of all the things that could go wrong as a result of the marriage. Could I have kids? What if I could not walk tomorrow? I knew my strengths, but life is unpredictable. For now, it was safer to keep it to just friendship. I was living the life of my dreams and I wanted to keep things the way they were.

Sometimes my friends and family would call me aside and ask me why I did not want to pressure Tony to marry me since they could tell he loved me. I would tell them we were just having a great time and if the relationship ended the next day I would still be grateful. They told me I was going to be dumped soon if I did not force him to put a ring on my finger, he would soon abandon me and move on. Truly, and the Lord knows I mean it, if Tony had moved on, I would not have begrudged him, he already gave me the greatest gift of all.

He showed me that I was worthy of love just the way I was.

One rule I had was if he was staying, he needed to treat me with utmost respect. It would be a huge disaster for anyone living with disability to coerce another to marry them. I was very aware of my circumstances, though they did not stop me, I knew they were there.

Back to life in Port Harcourt, I just received a letter that my bank would like to interview me for a permanent position in the legal department. They gave me a date that was two weeks away, I was elated. I knew I would have the chance to see Tony again, since it was in Lagos and also I was confident that the bank would retain me. As the day drew closer, I travelled by air to Lagos; Tony was there to meet me. As usual it was always a thrill to see him. Early the next day I took time to dress up. I wore a beautiful black suit with a white silk shirt, my thick black hair was pulled back in a ponytail, the only jewelry I wore was my pair of diamond studs. I completed the look with black patent Ferragamo pumps. I made my way to the magnificent building on No 1 Kingsway Road in Ikoyi. I went through security and was directed to the sixth floor, as I made it to the elevators, I took time to observe the bankers milling around the banking hall; they were all well-dressed, they all looked professional. I was very confident; I was not intimidated. Just thought to myself, 'soon I will be one of them.'

I got to the sixth floor, there was a conference room at the end of the hall and opposite the door were a few young people like me waiting to be interviewed. One by one the young people were ushered into the conference room, soon it was my turn. I walked through the door and what I saw made my heart sink. My initial reaction was to turn back and leave, but that would be out of character for me. There were about ten panelists and as I dragged my weak leg into the room, I saw them exchanging glances, like what is someone like this doing here? I knew I had to take back control. Taking control here would involve bringing the issue of disability on the table and discussing it.

The practice then was that after the introductions, you would be asked to tell the panel about yourself. I was asked this question and this was my answer:

"My name is Chinwe Anyaehie. One word that I love, is the word challenge. I was born with cerebral palsy which in some way has challenged me, but I have mastered how to turn around the things that challenge me to my advantage. I enjoy seeking out challenges and tackling them. I sought a career that would bring that challenge. Law did that for me and now banking is my next territory to conquer. I know you noticed my limp when I walked in, I saw the way some of you exchanged glances. Do not let that be a concern. I am quite capable." They claimed they did not notice it. I ended by telling them to look out for the limp on my way out, since they claimed they did not notice it on my way in. By the time I finished, they were in shock. The room was so quiet you could hear a pin drop. Then they said they were done, there were no further questions. I got up and took my leg with me. When I left the room, I wondered for a minute if I was a bit too direct, then I said to myself, "That was fun, I do not care if I got the job or not. I will apply to another bank if they don't take me."

The next day I flew back to Port Harcourt. A few days later a letter came in the mail, I was offered the position. It would be a while before anyone on that panel forgot me!

Things were really falling into place. On the personal level there were pros and cons to being away from Tony, the distance was killing me, but on the other hand it gave me the time to think things over. I really did not know how things were going to work out. The longer it lingered, I knew I was playing with fire. Thankfully my new job was there to take my mind off things and I tried to focus. One thing though, I kept all my dreams alive, especially the one about the house full of kids, beautiful girls and boys. The dream about the children was safer to entertain than that of a husband. Sometimes, I felt it would be better to marry a non-Nigerian, may be someone from Europe or the United States, someone from a place that was kinder to people with disabilities. This relationship was sadly not going to be between Tony and myself. There was a society that had an interest, it would be like being in a multi-racial relationship in a society that was divided along color lines, there would be people outside of the parties that would take it very personally.

In all fairness to Tony's family, they had all accepted the fact that he was in a relationship with me, they all treated me with dignity and respect. My favorite member of his family was his grandma. When his mom was being conferred with a chieftaincy title, Tony had asked me to attend the event with him. I travelled with him to his maternal home and on getting there, I met his grandparents; they were so warm and accommodating. The first thing his grandma said to me was about whether or not I was going to marry her grandson. Tony and his Mom screamed at the same time. They let her know the relationship was fresh and that were good friends. She said she was just asking. Tony's Grandpa was a soft spoken, slim man, he had very light skin like he was mixed, his hair was snow white in color, he spoke very little to me, but I could tell he was a man of peace. On the other hand, his grandma was very dark, tall, and thick; she was the exact opposite of her husband, but they were very similar in their kind hearts. She was bold and not afraid to speak her mind. We spent a couple of days in his village and then I returned back to base.

On my way home, I wondered what type of family this was, everybody was so nice. I thought of his grandma and smiled, she was something else. For the first time, I thought of her question and smiled. It felt good to know that she thought of me as someone that stood a chance as a woman. It was one of those things you said to yourself, when you were being truthful to self, but that you never admit to anyone that you felt that way.

Orianu, or Nma Nnukwu as they called her, made me feel worthy more than any other person in that family. There was another incident with her years later, after we had our first son, Chidera. Tony's mother lived in the United States at this time and as is customary, when you have a child, the mother or female members of the family, would come and do what we call "onugwo." They would teach the new mom how to take care of the new born and help nurse the mother back to health. On my side of the family, my mom came for a few days and left and then my sister Lizzy came in her place, on Tony's side his grandma was overjoyed, she was the one most suited to come, moreover she was a big fan of mine. I had also given birth to her first great grandchild. Something happened that made me love this old woman even more. After the baby, I was asked to abstain from intimacy for six weeks. As a first time mother I wanted to obey all the rules, Tony was not happy about this particular rule. Initially he was excited over the birth of his son, eventually he became very cranky and instead of the usual loving Tony he huffed and puffed all over the place.

Nma Nnukwu called me and asked when was the last time we were intimate. I told her the doctor wanted me to abstain for six weeks. She told me my husband was not too happy about that and that she could tell. She told me to give him some attention. I obeyed and the next morning the usual Tony was back. Nma noticed the next morning. She whispered to me that it looks like I obeyed her. I told her yes and she gave me the thumbs up. She was so wise.

Back to Port Harcourt, after that trip to his maternal home, I really did not want to stay so far away, moreover there were things happening at work that I did not really like; I was looking for every reason to move to Lagos. My thinking was changing, in the months that followed I planned to relocate. I was not going to do it suddenly; I was going to plan it.

13

THE BOLD STEP

I came to the realization that the relationship was not going to work if we were apart, it was easier for me to move to Lagos than for Tony to leave his mom and come to Port Harcourt.

I could easily secure a job with another bank, so I packed up a few things, told my little girl Mercy I would be gone for a short while I left her with my Sister Lizzy and I went to Lagos. I truly do not believe I would have the life I have now if I had not made that move. I always say, "we know our true desires even when we would not admit it to others." I talk to myself a whole lot and I put my cards out on the table, strategy and planning goes a long way. I was very aware of my desires, but I was also aware that they may not be attainable for someone like me. Was I going to stop living based on this truth? My answer was no, but I was going to proceed with caution and be prepared for whatever the future brought. Dating a person living with disabilities is not easy for either party. The one living with disabilities has to face facts and understand that it is going to be a huge challenge on the other party and allow them the liberty of thinking the consequences through, while the other party had to be considerate, fair, and truthful. If you get to the point where you cannot continue the relationship, be open and fair by letting the other person know, do not play games nor lie about your difficulty to continue. I guess these rules apply to every other relationship. I was in a great relationship, if it worked and matured into a marriage, great! If not, I would gladly move on, because of this understanding and the conscious effort not to pressure Tony, he started to relax. I always say Tony is human, but in my eyes, he can do no wrong. Anyone that can commit to a relationship like ours at twenty-one years of age is an exceptional person. Tony Iro is my hero.

As soon as I got to Lagos, I started looking for a place, I wanted my own place, but I wanted it close to where Tony lived. This area was called Festac. By this time Tony was doing well as a real estate lawyer, he helped me find a rental property. It was a four-bedroom duplex and had two living rooms and a dining room. This was my second home so I knew exactly how to make it look amazing. It was beautiful. The décor reflected who I was and where I was in life, it reflected my truth. One of the rooms was a nursery, I was ready to be a mother. This dream never left me even when the dream of a husband did not seem realistic. I was a lawyer, I had my own house. I was my own woman. Once that nursery was set up I knew exactly what I wanted to do.

Tony and I continued seeing each other, by this time the relationship was about into the fourth year. We did everything together, sometimes he would spend time in my place other times I would go over to his house, it was better to leave things exactly as they were. There was no need to change anything. "If it is not broken why fix it?" However, life is not always that simple even if you leave everything as it is, life will happen. There was pressure mounting everywhere. Even my family felt I was ruining my chances of marrying another man if he did not marry me.

You two are already a couple, he acts like he loves you dearly, so why are you not making him commit? I knew the answer, yet I was afraid to admit it...I was afraid! The question here is, afraid of what? I was afraid for him, I felt he did not truly know what he was getting into and I felt obligated as his lover to protect him from my life and my circumstances.

Several times I prayed and wished he would get a life and move on. I knew I did not have the strength to go, but I wished he would make it easier on us and leave.

On his end there was the pressure from his loved ones and friends (except my mother-in-law and his grandmother) that the relationship that started out as a joke was dangerously developing into something very serious and they were uncomfortable with that, they felt he should get out of the relationship now before it was too late. I could see where they were coming from, but there was nothing I could do about it, only Tony could help himself.

I cannot really speak for him concerning why he did not go. There was also the issue of danger in dating a guy like Tony. He was a great looking guy, doing very well, romantic, sensitive, and kind. He also called every woman sweetheart and left them drooling for more. Once these women knew he was dating me, they felt there was room for them to win him over. I was not bothered about that. I knew who I was and if he was going to walk so be it. I knew I was a huge asset to him or any other man. I left him with the liberty to stay or walk. Problem was, he was smitten. I already had him spellbound! All he needed was to look in my big brown eyes. To date, some daring women still think that they stand a chance with him—after all the wife is disabled, the poor guy must need a better woman.

While the desire to be married was steadily extinguished, the desire to have a child was getting stronger. I am extremely stubborn and if I want something I go for it.

One day we went out for lunch at a local restaurant. It was our regular, I liked their garri and onugbu soup. I was extremely skinny no one believed I ate garri regularly. We had just finished our meal and we were talking when I threw up all my food, something was terribly wrong, I never throw up. We apologized to the owner as they cleaned up and hurriedly left the place. I could tell Tony was concerned by the look on his face and how tightly he held my hand, I was hardly sick, this was unusual for me. He wanted me to go to the doctor, but I assured him I was okay. It never happened again and I did not think anything about it but I knew things were just not right.

I eventually listened to Tony and went to the doctor. The first thing he did was to order a pregnancy test; the results came back positive. We had mixed feelings. We were happy, but it brought all the fears to the surface. For me, I have wanted a child all my life, here is the chance, but I was not married. However, I was carrying a child for the best man on earth, I knew he was a good man, but I did not want him to feel pressured into marrying me because of the pregnancy.

Then there was the fear of how things would go with the pregnancy. What if something went wrong? My other worry was my parents. They were very traditional and this would be totally unacceptable. What was I to do now? Well it was a bit too late to think of all these things.

We decided to keep it to ourselves. No one could tell since I carried the pregnancy so well. Soon days became weeks and months. We were not born again Christians at this time so I did not really feel any guilt from the pregnancy.

One day Tony came to my place and asked if we could pray. He prayed for us and for the relationship and he asked God to show him a sign that I was the right choice for him. After the prayer, he told me that he respected my decision to have the child and that he was opposed to having any child out of wedlock. He told me he would like very much to marry me, but he wanted me to be patient, in the meantime he wanted me to move in with him so he could take proper care of me.

As the pregnancy progressed I developed cold feet. What if things did not work out like I wanted them to? I loved this man to the moon and back, but loving him was not enough to not worry about what type of marriage we would have when we were out of the honeymoon stage. My worst fear was what if during an argument in the future he tells me he did me a favor by marrying me and he would not have married me if I hadn't been pregnant. That would really make me angry because I believed that I was an asset. This is very common, whenever you see a marriage with a spouse living with disability, people say things like God bless the other person for marrying this person with their disabilities, as if the disabled partner is worthless and really has nothing to offer.

I know who I am, I knew that I would be an asset to any man as a wife, but sadly things are not that logical in the world, and I would hate to go into the marriage and watch Tony act like he was shortchanged. However, I had known this man for some time and he had proven his love over and over, if things did not work out then it would not be the first marriage that did not work out; I would continue in my journey.

Once a month we would take a trip to First Consultants Hospital in Lagos to see the doctor for prenatal checks. Every visit Tony was by my side. It was becoming a reality, this motherhood dream. There was one other issue, the issue of telling my parents. I was not ignorant of the fact that my parents did not know I was pregnant. I came from a very traditional family and there was no way they would be happy that I was pregnant without getting married first. I know my dad would accuse Mama of giving me too many liberties. They would regret letting me live on my own at such a young age. Well it was kind of too late to worry about all that now.

Sonograms were not done in those days unless you had complications so we did not know the sex of the child. Regardless, we started planning, first we needed a name. We decided that the name should be Chidera no matter the sex. Igbo names are unique in the sense that they tell a story. Chidera is a name that says it all, literally it means "Whatever God has written, will definitely come to pass." The Lord had written this unique story indeed. This girl that has been deemed worthless would have a child. God has written it and it was about to come to pass.

We were taking things one day at a time, not thinking too deeply about the consequences of our actions. Christmas came around and it was the practice for most Igbo people to travel back to their hometown. My hometown Nkwerre was the best place to be at Christmas, I would not miss it for anything, but if I went back home, there was no way Mama's prying eyes would not detect the pregnancy. If I had to travel home, I would have to come up with some explanation. Well, I would cross that bridge when I got there.

Having a pregnant girlfriend brought out an even better side of Tony, he was a natural at care giving, he was always by my side, spoiling and pampering me; sometimes it would get a little on my nerves because I wanted a bit of space, but I enjoyed every bit of the attention he gave me.

One day he came over to my house and he said he wanted us to say a special prayer, we both knelt down and he prayed. In his prayer, he told God he was about to make a decision and that he wanted God to show him if this was the right decision for us. As he prayed, I listened silently, a part of me was tickled, I thought to myself, this handsome young man is considering me for marriage. Me! WOW! The one that had always been looked at as a factory reject…even if he did not go through with it, I was already flattered at the consideration. On the other hand, I was scared. If he went through with it, it would not be easy, there will be a lot of opposition, these conflicting thoughts danced around in my mind as he drew the prayer to an end. My self-talk again: "Chinwe, do not let your imagination run wild."

After the prayer, things moved at full speed, I guess he got the answers he sought from God. As Christmas came, I travelled home. I had no clue what was waiting for me as I was busy hiding my slightly widened waistline from Mama. I was able to do this, since I hardly added any weight and my stomach did not protrude like that of other women in their sixth month of pregnancy, but her eyes followed me around, like she suspected something. Once, she casually said I looked like I added a few pounds, I just smiled and moved away from her.

One afternoon, someone came and informed me that Tony was there to see me, my heart leaped and I made my way downstairs to the entry to receive him and bring him upstairs. It was taboo to entertain a man you were not married to in the family home, luckily my parents were out and my siblings already knew who Tony was.

We made it to one of the living rooms upstairs and I was very happy to see him. We hugged and kissed as he looked me over, making sure I was doing well. We wanted a little bit of privacy so we stepped out to the balcony, there were double glass sliding doors leading to the balcony and I closed the doors behind us. Once we were settled in the balcony, Tony got down on one knee and took my left hand. I was confused, what was going on? Then he started, "Chinwe Anyaehie, will you marry me?" My heart was beating very fast and I was trying so hard to process what was going on. I said, "Yes!" He slipped the ring on my finger. It was a yellow gold ring with onyx and diamonds all around it.

My thoughts were going all over the place. When did he get the ring? How did he know my size and how long had he been planning this? As

I toyed with these questions, Tony stood up, pulled me toward him and we kissed passionately. I was going to be Mrs. Chinwe Iromuanya. How exciting! I was going to marry my friend! I was going to be a wife and a mother! He wanted me for keeps! He loved me enough to risk all! And then the opposite emotions took over. How would this work? Would he regret marrying a wife with one bad leg in the future? Would he want more later? Could he handle the stares and negative comments that were bound to come? Would I be enough? I guess it was too late to ask these questions, he just asked and I just said yes.

Saying yes and slipping a ring on my finger was one thing, he still had to get consent from my family and perform the customary rights to take me as a wife. Tony said he wanted to do the customary marriage while we were home for Christmas, before we returned to base so we would not have to travel back later.

My parents had met him a few times before, but they did not know we were in a very serious relationship.

He approached my Mum and told her that he wanted my hand in marriage and he wanted to perform the customary rights as soon as possible, he told her he intended to come back with his people in a few days, he told her the day and requested a list of requirements.

Mama was elated, but she kept her joy under control, just like when you go to inspect a home that meets all your requirements and you have to keep calm and act like you are not excited. She gave him the list, but also let him know she would tell Chief of his intentions when he came home.

After Tony left, Mama called me for a talk, she asked me if this was what I wanted to do? I told her yes, that I loved him and that he was a wonderful man. She smiled and told me she liked him too, at this time, I confided in her that I was over six months pregnant. Her eyes widened and she told me that my dad must not hear of the pregnancy or there would be no traditional wedding. In my custom, you do not have a ceremony for a woman already pregnant, you just hand her over to the man with no ceremony, she is considered to have given of her virtue prematurely.

When my dad came home, Mama told him about Tony and his intentions and his desire to come back in a few days and he told her he was happy for me and that he would be glad to entertain Tony and his people, but not on the date they had chosen. Of course Mama did not mention the pregnancy, we were going to keep that a secret until after the ceremony.

There was just one problem, this was not the days of cell phones, there was no way to tell Tony not to come on the day he said he would for the ceremony.

On that day, he assembled the selected members of his family to go get his bride, when he got to my home, Mama informed him that the ceremony could not happen that day, Chief had chosen a new date. Tony was not too happy about that, he let Mama know that. Mama in her loving peaceful way calmed him down and let him know that my dad had to put a little bit of a hurdle so that he would appreciate how special his bride is.

Tony calmed down, spent some time with me, and left.

On the 4th of January, the love of my life returned with a bigger delegation, by the time they got to my compound, they were welcomed by my dad and my extended family. They were expecting them and this time they were received in one of the reception halls in the compound.

I dressed up in one of my mum's traditional outfits, the one I chose was a loose top and wrapper, also called Iro and Buba. I wore the blouse over the wrapper so that it would conceal my slightly protruding tummy. Soon the negotiations were done between the families, it was time to present the items on the list, it included things like tobacco, assorted drinks, cola nuts, but no money as my dad excluded money whenever he gave any of his daughters away.

Toward the end of the ceremony, some palm wine was poured in a local cup, handed to me. Dad addressed me. He told me that a person was there for my hand in marriage, he said if I knew the person in the crowd that I wanted to be married to, I should take a sip of the palm wine and find my husband in the crowd and bring my choice to him. I was very nervous, I took a sip of the drink and searched around the room for Tony, I found him, handed him the drink and brought him to my dad. The crowd cheered and my father presented us to the family and blessed the union. It was time to celebrate. There was a lot of food and drinks, one drink that made quite an impression was the local palm wine from my husband's people. Mmanyi Ndi Umuahia—The palm wine of Umuahia—like my people called it. The wine was so different from that of my village, it was so smooth and sweet, everyone in my family complimented the drink. Until the day my mother died, she talked about that wine.

While we dined, I could not believe how fast things had progressed. I was now Mrs. Chinwe Iromuanya. I turned and looked at my husband; we were just babies, he looked so young. I could not help but wonder if we would have a successful marriage. Twenty-four years later, I think back and admit that we made the best decision. It is not perfect, we have had our fair share of trials, but God has been kind, we are still together.

14

CHIDERA - FULFILLMENT OF GOD'S PROMISE

fter the excitement of Christmas and the traditional marriage, we returned to Lagos ready to tackle life together. I settled in to making Tony's family house comfortable and conducive for a new baby; we started planning in earnest for the new baby. The days were flying by and one day, one of my aunties came to visit us and I told her I felt like I would have the baby

soon. Something was different that day, my stomach was very flat and it looked like the baby had moved to the lower part of my stomach. She asked me to show her my stomach and she burst out laughing, she said I did not even look pregnant and not to talk about being due. My aunty had about eight children so I believed her. When it was time for us to take my aunty home, I asked Tony, if we could stop at the hospital to refill my prenatal supplements and he said yes. We stopped at the First Consultants on our way to my aunty's house and we went into the consulting room to talk to the doctor about the refill.

My doctor, a Russian lady married to a Nigerian—I believe her name was Dr. Aregbesele—told me that because I was past thirty-six weeks, she had to examine me. I had an elective cesarean section scheduled to take place in two weeks; I had scheduled it because my family felt that would be safer considering my disability.

Dr. Aregbesele had examined me earlier and told me my pelvis was in excellent condition and that she saw no reason I could not have the baby vaginally, but I did not want to take the risk. After the doctor told me that I could have the baby naturally if I chose, I asked Tony if he felt I could do it and he said, "Of course." His answer gave me strength. I tapped into his strength, but in our usual way, we prayed and told God that since the elective caesarean section was scheduled at thirty-eight weeks, if it was his wish that I should have the baby naturally he should make me go into labor before the day.

So, on the day we took my aunty home, the doctor examined me and screamed. Even though the surgery was scheduled three days from that day, I was in full labor. She said I was six centimeters dilated and fully effaced, she said the baby would be here the next few hours and that I needed to go straight to the labor ward. As she walked us out, she saw my aunty, she asked her why she could not tell I was in labor. Aunty said it was because I did not look pregnant.

I went to the labor room which was on the top floor, when I got there, the nurses asked me why I was there? I told them my doctor had asked me to come up. They asked if I was pregnant and I said yes, they did not believe me, but they went ahead and started preparing me for delivery. The nurses commented on my appearance, the fact that I was so flat in the stomach and that I was too calm and well put together to be in labor. I had my huge earrings on and my usual red lipstick.

Soon the doctor was up to deliver the baby, a little after she came in, I delivered this handsome healthy baby boy. Chidera Anthony Iromuanya. Tony and I had chosen the name as soon as we knew we were pregnant, the name was one that reflected our circumstances, it was one that we chose in faith believing that God would fulfill his promises. Chidera means "what God has written, no man can stop."

April, 1994, we welcomed our first son into the world. I could see the joy on Tony's face as he stared at this wonderful gift, he held my hand and kissed me over and over, trying unsuccessfully to hold back his tears. Soon they were taking the baby to the nursery and Tony followed them to make sure nothing went wrong.

I process things a little differently; I do not show my emotions easily for fear of being found weak. I was praising God and thanking him for making this possible for me to be a mother. "This is an impossible that just became possible." I was having the most beautiful dream and I did not want anyone to wake me up. I have had this dream from the time I was a little girl and now it was reality. Once our son was born, we quickly inspected his hands, legs, fingers, and toes and they were all perfect. There were just too many emotions dancing around in my head. I was elated.

As the doctors and nurses were cleaning me up, the doctor said she had never had a labor so fast, she cautioned us that going forward we had to be careful when we were ready to have another baby because I was one of the women blessed with a condition called precipitated labor and that it gets worse as you have more children. She said in subsequent pregnancies I had to be extremely careful because I could have the baby on the street if I was out and about in late pregnancy.

To describe how I felt after Chidera's delivery would be very difficult to put in words, I was overwhelmed with gratitude. Every day after we got home from the hospital I would follow this beautiful perfect child with my eyes wondering if this was truly my child or if I was in one of my day dreams that was yet to manifest. In my language we say, "when God gives a child a present that is too big, the child will ask who it is meant for." (Enye nwata ihe ka ya, ya si, isi m nye onye?) This present was too big for me to believe. I was practically waiting for the owner of the child to come claim him. Days after coming home, my husband went to inform all the neighbors that his wife had just delivered a bouncing baby boy and they asked if I was pregnant. He thought that statement to be so absurd as he wondered what they had thought, but we actually knew where that was coming from. Due to the overflow of joy we felt in our hearts we had no time to waste on negative emotions. Looking back now I understand why it was so hard for any one that knew me to believe that I could carry a child to term in the most inconspicuous way; they expected to see some kind of burden on me as the pregnancy progressed, instead I had an extremely flat stomach and there was no discomfort from the pregnancy.

In the days that followed our return, family from all parts of the country were making trips to Lagos to see things for themselves. Could it really be true? Maybe she had the child 'with operation' like they say in Nigeria, which meant caesarean section. Maybe a surrogate carried the baby to term and they went to the hospital and pretended to bring back their baby. There were just too many versions of the story, some informed us about their disbelief while others just talked about it behind our backs, the few that believed were giving thanks to God. Daily news of the birth spread everywhere. One day Tony had gone for a meeting with a real estate client, it was a client he had met through one of my cousins in the past, but he did not remember her. As he got to the meeting, the lady said she knew who

Tony was and went further to describe how she knew him. She said my cousin's name and said Tony was the guy that was deceiving that girl with the bad leg, (that seems to be the way Nigerians like to describe anyone with any form of disability in the legs) Tony asked her who she was talking about? She confirmed she was talking of me. He went further to tell her I was his wife and that we just had a son, the lady did not believe him and he eventually convinced her and she suddenly said she had something to tell him and that he was welcome to ask my cousin about it.

She then told him that my cousin said there was no way Tony was going to marry me because the doctor's had confirmed that I could not carry a baby to term and that she knew Tony being so young, was definitely going to want his own children. My husband came back so dejected, but decided not to ask my cousin, we just wanted to focus on our lives and build a family.

Family continued to come as is our tradition. Tony's grandma came first, his mom was residing in the United States at the time, but she was overjoyed. This was the first grandson of Michael Iromuanya's family. It was emotional for her, her husband had been killed during the Nigerian civil war and with all the challenges that herself and her children had experienced after the death of her husband, it was a miracle to see the first grandchild. She sent loads of gifts from America, greeting cards and money for the baby. She also sent a name, as is tradition even if the parents of the child name him, the grandparents will do the same. She called him Amamdi meaning "my lineage is alive," that was how Ama got his name. Going down memory lane there was a gift from Grandma Rose that I will never forget. It was a beaded waist coat with an elephant on the back, that waist coat was simply amazing. Whenever Ama wore the waist coat, people stopped us on the streets to compliment him. The first time Ama wore the waist coat was at our court wedding. Grandma Rose was a very artistic and creative person, she had a very distinct and wonderful taste in fashion. She was also extremely beautiful. She was a showstopper any day. She had also sent him this tiny gold ring. Whenever we went to church Ama wore his ring.

However, Grandma Rose could not come to visit immediately after the birth of Ama, so Tony's grandma came in her place. On her arrival, she danced around thanking God that she had lived to see the birth of another generation. Orianu as her children and grandchildren called her was a beautiful soul, she was a combination of inner beauty and deep spirituality. She knew it all. I got my one big lesson on how to take care of a man from Orianu. It was during this same period that she came to see her first great-grandson, Chidera. She noticed that my husband looked irritated and frustrated and that was out of character for him, since Tony is always in a joyous mood. One day she observed him snap at me and Orianu pulled me aside and said, "Nne when was the last time you had any form of intimacy with my grandson?" I looked at her in amazement as I reminded her that the doctor had recommended abstinence for at least six weeks and this was just the third week. She asked me what I was going to do about my current problems. I told her I did not know how to handle them. She thought real hard and then started to speak to me in hush tones, she said she not trying to discredit my doctor, but my husband needed me right now. She advised me to make myself available to my husband that night and that I would see a change in the morning. That night, I put her advice into practice and it worked like magic.

On coming down the steps the next morning, I met Orianu on the landing of the stairs. After exchanging the usual morning greetings, she had a glint of mischief in her eyes as she lowered her voice and asked, "Did you carry out my instructions?" I said "Yes, Ma." That was not all, soon Tony came down the stairs in very high spirits, whistling. Orianu's eyes caught mine and she smiled and gave me a thumbs up. Oh my! Orianu may be old, but she was not out of practice. She sure knows what it took to win a man's heart.

Armed with Orianu's advice, it was not a surprise that in a very short time, I found out I was pregnant again.

15

SOMTOCHUKWU

*H*istory was repeating itself as we were celebrating being pregnant a second time. Som's pregnancy was sort of different. We were doing it the right way this time, there was no secrecy like we experienced during Chidera's pregnancy.

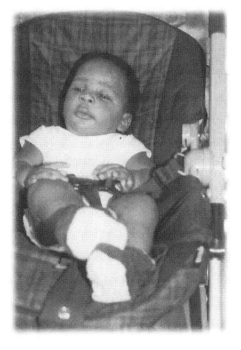

I had done this once before, so the experience was not completely new to me. Days rolled into weeks and weeks into months, it was the same pattern, I hardly looked pregnant again, no one other than members of our immediate families who we told, could tell we were expecting. My stomach was very flat and I had added just a few more pounds. I had excessive energy and I had no problem carrying myself and the baby around. I believe the reason most people doubted each time I was pregnant was because they were expecting to see just a little bit of difficulty in my ability to carry the baby, so when they saw me jumping around and wearing the same type clothes I wore when I was not pregnant, they didn't have any reason to think another baby was on the way.

Once in a while, I found myself retreating to my quiet corner, the one I usually escaped to when I needed to daydream and whenever I had a moment to be there. I would wonder, what in the name of God was going on? Did God just decide to bless me beyond my wildest imagination? Sometimes I would think that I was in a dream and someone may wake me up any moment.

There was no reason to daydream, I was living my dream. Often, I would remember my journey and what it has taken for me to get here. Every step of my existence, I had to try so hard to let others know that I was a living breathing thing. All the days and nights of doubts, the stares, yes those stares that felt like daggers going in and out of my stomach, and those staring not realizing how much it bothered me. I remember the endless side talks that people made while making poor attempts to whisper in my presence. I remember the ugly words I heard from people when they were not too happy with me. I remember this family friend that met me one day, fighting for my rights as I always did, and how he said to me that he wondered why I could not keep my mouth shut and accept how people treated me, that after all I was not well. That was typical Nigerian mentality toward anyone living life with any form of challenges. They called them 'the sick one.' I am a very healthy person, but that does not stop them from calling me a sick person.

As Somto's pregnancy grew, my worry grew less and less. I guess with Chidera's case I was not sure if that was just a one-time blessing, but watching it happen a second time did something to me. Please let no one wake me up from this very beautiful sleep. We found out I was pregnant with Somto a few months before Chidera's first birthday. By the time of Chidera's birthday celebration—which was a huge Birthday party that led to the closure of our streets—most of the guests had no clue our second son was already on the way.

I took time to articulate these thoughts and feeling, hoping that someone somewhere in their personal struggles would find them helpful and step out in faith to pursue their dreams.

My prayer is that these stories would heal me and also others. Personally I have found much healing in going back to re-live my experiences at these times.

Sometimes, my joy would be replaced with fear as I wondered if the Lord would be merciful to let my motherhood experiences this time be just as beautiful and smooth as before. There was always that doubt as number two progressed. We were about five months into Som's pregnancy, when the mailman delivered a letter from my sister, Ihuoma, she lived in the United States. I had not kept in touch with her since we got married, but I had no doubt that Mama kept her updated on our news. Ihuoma lived in Dallas and there was a visa lottery program that allowed professionals living in Africa to migrate to the United States and be granted permanent residency under the DVI program. The visa lottery would have to be entered by someone living in the United States. My sister had entered the names of all our family members and guess whose name was drawn? My name. So the mailman brought this big package at a time we were living the life of our dreams. By this time, I had put my artistic skills in great practice by redecorating Tony's family house. It was a beautiful home for us and our child. I remember the living room with the white wallpaper that had embossed palm like prints, this covered the upper part of the room and the lower part was paneled in strips of pine wood, meticulously lined.

The floor was diagonally shaped tiles, that were ordered from Italy by his mum years before. There were big windows all around the living room. Labor was cheap in Lagos, so to do any form of remodeling was not much of a hassle. Just before Chidera was born, we had the wallpaper painted over in white, this made the room appear even larger and to make it even more interesting we created the illusion of two living rooms by using two different styles of décor. On one end, we had modern upholstered furniture covered in thick off-white cotton fabric piped in pink, I remember that the choice of color became a problem at the entrance of a boisterous baby like Chidera, who was very active as a baby. He was the king of his domain, he controlled everything and everyone in our home, quite different from his very reserved demeanor now. Anyway back to the living room, the setting with the upholstered off-white furniture faced the window that looked to the gate. You could see any one coming into the house from that part of the living room. On the other side of the room, just by the huge glass sliding doors, was the contrast sitting. This we accomplished by having very roomy rattan furniture, made of dark colored cane, woven into an intricate pattern, unlike most rattan furniture made in those days that had a weak wooden base we made these sturdy by making the base from strong, thick iron.

The seat and back were covered in a light green fabric that had small flowers all over. We limited the seating on this side to two roomy arm chairs to give easy access to the courtyard on the other side of the glass doors. When you sat on this side of the living room, you had a clear view of the courtyard and the spiral staircase leading upstairs. One thing I could say about Tony's mom was that she put in a lot of thought and planning into the building. It was a beautiful house, this made decorating easy.

As you walked through the wooden front doors, there was yet another spiral staircase leading upstairs to a huge master suite. This staircase was made out of big rocks like you were entering a cave. When we lived there, we put all her belongings in the master suite since she lived there. We kept this section of the house out of bounds. Opposite her section of the house were the bedrooms, there were about three of them in a row. We made a nursery in one of the bedrooms. The nursery had primary colored wooden furniture and the way we decorated was to accommodate multiple children and the choice of furniture was such, that it transitioned with the children as they grew. Truly my mindset at that time was, that if God kept blessing us the way he was, with smooth pregnancies and deliveries we were going to have a house full of little Chinwes and Tonys running all over the place. We had enough household help and life was great. so why not? Anyway. before I get off track, let me return to the current pregnancy which is Somto's and the letter from the United States immigration congratulating us on our winning the visa lottery. In the big envelope were instructions concerning the processes we had to follow to be found eligible to migrate to the States. One of the requirements was a marriage certificate. We realized that may be a bit problematic since the only marriage we had was the native law and customs. Remember we were pregnant with Chidera at that time and then after his birth we had to settle down as a couple and take care of a lot of things. The house and our household staff were adjusting to the introduction of a new baby.

There was one thing after the other. Our plan was that once we were settled, we would have a huge wedding. This visa lottery added a new wrinkle, as we considered the requirements, we sat down and discussed if we wanted to relocate to the United States. We considered the new opportunities that would be there for young Chidera and the baby we were expecting. We considered better educational opportunities and security. We were afraid of giving up our comfort zone, but agreed that in the interest of our children it was a sacrifice worth making.

Once we decided we were making the move, we needed to plan a small wedding at the wedding registry in Ikeja. We agreed on a date, August 29th which was Tony's birthday; it was just round the corner. We started informing our family and friends of our intentions. First we called his mom and then my parents just to let them know what we planned, we knew they could not make it. Tony's mom was resident in the U.S. at the time and my parents were in London. Due to the short notice, we did not expect them to come back. So I informed my sister, Ndidi. Ndy and I have always had a very unique relationship, she is always there for me and vice versa. She is just three years older. She was my major supporter at this time, she believed so much in me and my abilities and there was no way we could be planning a wedding without letting Ndy know. So I placed a call to Big Sis and told her we were planning a wedding, she was overjoyed. She went straight into "mama bear" mode, she wanted to know if I had something to wear. Ndy owns one of the biggest designer stores in Lagos and travelled all over the world attending fashion shows, collecting high end pieces. I told her because of the pregnancy I should wear one of my own dresses. She asked if we would have a lot of guests and I let her know, she would cater to them. We told her we wanted it very modest.

Tony on his end, informed his godfather who we called Daddy. Daddy was godfather extraordinaire, he understood the duties and responsibilities of being a godfather. At this time, we had very little family support, Daddy was there all the way. He was in the hospital immediately after Chidera was born and made daily home visits after that to make  sure we were doing okay. Daddy was the father figure in Tony's life. Then there was the very reliable Sister Lizzy, my other big sister, the Omugwo, which is the role that an older family member plays when a baby is born to a younger family member; for most people their mums play this role. The older family member teaches you how to take care of the new baby while taking care of you. Everything Tony and I know about baby care, Sister Lizzy taught us.

I remember the first few nights after bringing Chidera home, Sister Lizzy would give him his night bath and feed him while Tony watched. Tony watched because he intended to take over this role from Sister Lizzy

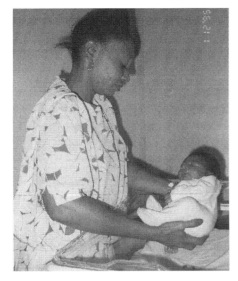

when she left. I did not pay much attention. I did not think I would ever be the one taking care of the children.

I remember one night, the baby was ready for bed, dressed in his blue and white sleeper, she laid him down on his bassinet by our bed, she covered the little bassinet with the mosquito netting to ward off the very vicious Lagos mosquitoes, and asked us to get some sleep too. She returned a few hours later to check in on us. We were both sitting by the bed, watching the baby. We were too afraid to sleep for fear of something going wrong.

That night, she gave us a lesson that stuck, she said, "If you two want to stay up and watch him like hawks, for fear that something may go wrong, you can do so. But you should say your prayers, commit him to the hands of God, and he will be there when you wake up." We reluctantly took her advice prayed for the baby and retired. From that day forward, we worried less about the baby.

So no surprise she was the next person in line to tell about the wedding. She was the same sister whose husband died when I was in law school. She had a kind heart, whenever we needed help she showed up on very short notice. We knew she would be there again when the new baby came. Then we sent out a few more invitations, there was Mark Mordi, Tony's best friend from college, Gloria Dike who was a good friend and lived a few houses away, there was my cousin Nne. So on the 29th of August, we made

the short trip to the Ikeja registry where we were greeted by friends and family and signed the dotted lines, the number one witness being our one-and-a-half-year-old son, Chidera. He looked so handsome with his fresh haircut and beaded waist coat that his Grandma had

sent him earlier from the United States. Now we had a marriage certificate to prove our marriage. Between the two of us, this was mere formality; we were already married and we took our vows to each other seriously.

Shortly after the wedding at the registry, we submitted our application to the United States embassy and waited for an interview date. On one of my visits to the doctor, she had informed me that I was in full labor at about twenty-seven weeks and she was a bit worried about that. She said from the sonogram she could tell it was another boy and that boys do not do very well when born premature. She suggested giving me some medication to slow my contractions and also to develop the baby's lungs, so

if I ended up having him early, he would have a better chance of survival. Tony and I were scared. We did not want to have this child early knowing that my cerebral palsy was caused mostly by that reason, but we prayed for close to ten weeks that was needed to get the baby out of the danger zone. My doctor made us understand she would feel most comfortable if the baby made it to at least thirty-six weeks. By this time, we had become born again. We decided we were going to ask God for one day at a time. Every morning, when we got up and we were still pregnant, we would say a prayer. "Dear God, thank you for today, please give us tomorrow." Day by day the Lord answered and we were grateful. I still did not know why the doctor was worried, I was not having any contractions in my own understanding since, I was not in any form of pain. At this point, the doctor had suggested limiting my activities and increase my weekly visits. I just stayed home, but I pretty much kept my activity level the same, stomach was still very flat and the thought of me being almost seven months pregnant and looking the way I did fascinated a lot of people. We kept the weekly visits and on one of those visits around the thirty-sixth week, she let us know that just like with the last baby, I was seven centimeters dilated and fully effaced. Letting me carry on with the baby under those conditions would be very risky, especially since I did not know when I was contracting, she said the baby was in a safer zone and she would recommend breaking my water and getting things started. We were better prepared this time, we already had everything we needed for the baby. Chidera had graduated to the big bed and we had the nursery decorated in Winnie the Pooh theme and had built a fresh drawer that we filled with well folded baby boys' clothes.

So we told her to go ahead, we were prepared; whenever we went for the weekly check-ups we would have my weekend bag in the trunk of the car. It had my nightgowns and matching dressing gowns with slit in the chest area to allow for easy breastfeeding, the bag had nursing bras and pads as well as my toiletries. My hospital, First Consultants, provided supplies for the baby. So once again, I made the trip upstairs to the labor room as Tony made a quick dash to the car to fetch my weekend bag. Once we were settled in the labor room, they broke my membrane. About fifteen minutes later, I informed the nurses that I felt like the baby was coming. They quickly fetched my doctor and he examined me and was surprised that I was truly ready.

Moments later entered Somtochukwu Ahamefughi Iromuanya. Prince number two, I was yet again overtaken with emotions as I wondered what I had done to deserve such kindness and mercy from God. Tony was crying and kissing me all over, I could tell he was so, so proud of me. Most of these emotional times, play out like I am in a trance, like it was happening to someone else and I am observing it. The baby was huge, once they weighed him they announced that he was a little over nine pounds that was a surprise to us as he barely made it to thirty-six weeks. They said the steroid shots helped him with the weight gain in the last few weeks and the fact that I was genetically prone to having big babies helped too. They put him in a clear plastic box to weigh him and get his vital signs and he just filled up the box. Once they were done with the checks, they handed him to me. I examined this beautiful baby, he had a lot of curly hair and hair covered his entire body like he was a little chimp. I examined every part of the body as I tried so hard not to break down. He was a little darker in skin tone than his older brother, but I was in love all over again. I remember Tony asking me how we were going to split the tenderness in our heart for each cutie that came along, I told him we would figure it out. I guess it came naturally to us as we were able to give each child our hearts wholly and duplicate the same love for the next one without reducing the former.

I guess that is one of the things we took from God.

Baby Somto had no difficulty latching on, it was the days of the exclusive breastfeeding campaign and it was recommended that mothers got babies to latch on immediately after birth. Somto has always loved his food. Tony watched as he took his first feed. He looked too young to be the father of two children. He is such an incredible father and I thank God over and over again that this is the father of my sons. He does the job of fatherhood with ease, he was born to be a father. Soon they came to take the baby to the nursery and Tony followed to make sure they put the right name tag on the right baby. He returned with a smile, he informed me that Somto was the biggest baby in the nursery. He said Somto looked like King Kong and other babies were like his subjects, we laughed. What a day! I thought to myself. We could not thank God enough.

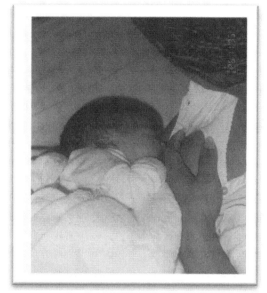

Soon the nurses cut into my thoughts by reminding me it was time to get some rest. I informed them I would do that after taking a good hot shower and changing into one of my pretty night dresses, they told me they did not recommend going into the shower as I was still weak from the labor. Of course, they did not know who they were talking to, once they left the room, I pulled out my toiletries, took my shower, and put on some sweet smelling fragrances and went back to the bed. Tony was tired and he had pulled out the sleeper by the bed and was already snoring.

The next morning, we were awakened by the entrance of several doctors and nurses, they had a serious look on their faces, our hearts sank as we waited patiently to hear what they had to say. They informed us that our son had jaundice. They informed us that this was quite a common condition where the liver filters bilirubin from the bloodstream and releases it into the intestinal tract. A newborn's immature liver often can't remove bilirubin quickly enough, causing an excess of bilirubin. Jaundice due to these normal newborn conditions is called physiologic jaundice, and it typically appears on the second or third day of life.

They informed me that they would not necessarily worry about this, but that because of the high levels on the baby they were going to keep him longer for observations. They told me I could return home the next day, but not with the baby; however, I was welcome to stay and nurse the baby at extra cost. By the time, they finished saying what they had to say, I was crying. Tony was by my side, trying to comfort me. Oh no! Not my perfect looking baby, I thought to myself. Was it something we did wrong? Was he going to be okay? I asked the doctors before they left the room to continue their rounds, they said they did not know yet but that the plan was to make sure the baby was fed regularly and continue to repeat the tests, that hopefully if the numbers started to come down they would let us take him home The nurses had wheeled the baby in, in his little plastic bed and once they were done with their information session, they took him to the nursery to start his treatment under a special light. Later that day, we decided to go visit him at the nursery. He had a black mask over his eyes, like the padded sleep masks used to block out the light. He was curled up in his plastic crib and he was stark naked. There was a special ultra violet light beaming over him. My heart tore in pieces, no, not our perfect looking baby. Tony had his arms around me as he silently squeezed my shoulders in solidarity. He knew when I was in this mood, I did not want to be preached to. After some time with the baby he gently led me back to my room. He informed me he had to make a quick dash home to replenish our supplies.

He returned hours later with the girl that lived with us, Ngozi. She is also my cousin, she had lived with me since I moved to Lagos, she moved with me when I got married. Ngozi simply loved us. At the moment, she was the only one we could entrust with Chidera's care. Her primary duty was Chidera, but she was finding it a bit overwhelming to take care of the baby and do the rest of her household chores. We had employed Eugene, a cook and steward, who was handling the cooking very well, and there was Mike my driver who was introduced to me by my friend, Popo. Tony's grandma had sent us another girl, Christiana, who was supposed to take care of Somto. I really did not get along very well with her, but she would work for now. I was happy Ngozi came to visit me and the new baby. I was also happy to see Chidera as he planted a wet kiss on my cheek. I examined him to make sure he was looked well; I had not seen him since the day I went for the weekly check to the hospital with the hope of returning home.

He looked well and he was so cute. Ngozi was hopping around excitedly, she wanted to see the new baby. I reached for the help button and a nurse appeared, I asked her if we could see the baby for a few minutes, she left the room and returned later with the baby. Ngozi held him in her arms and announced that he was so cute. I watched with pride and a little bit of worry. We had been praying for a miracle to happen so we could take him home soon. I needed to get home soon, not just to show off the new baby, but to get back to my usual routine. I was getting tired of being locked up in the hospital. The hospital told me that I had been discharged so I could leave and come back as I wished. Once Tony took me out for a ride, but I was not relaxed, I wanted to go back to the hospital just in case they needed me. Ngozi lowered the baby so Chidera could see him, she asked him to say Somto and all he could say in his little voice was, "Tom tom." That was how Somto got his nickname Tom Tom. The nurses returned to take him back to the nursery. Ngozi and Chidera spent some time with us and then Tony left to take them home. The next morning, during the ward round, the doctors happily informed me that Somto's numbers were down and that we could go home. I asked if it could go back up and they said no. I was very excited; God was so good to us. I packed up our belongings and we put the baby in the car seat and returned. I left home less than a week ago as a mother of one son and I returned as mother of two! I still could not get over it. Once we got home and settled in to our daily routine there was a lot of work to be done.

The American embassy had written back and they had given us an interview date. We had about a month to prepare for the interview.

16

TRANSITIONING FROM FRIENDS TO COUPLE

*E*verything for us was happening too fast, we were still very in love. Tony worked as a real estate attorney he had an office off the foyer and it was tastefully done. He had a secretary show up every morning and in the back of the house in the space designated to be a gym. He also ran a tailoring business, his tailors would report for work and head to the back of the house, where the business was located. The open room off the kitchen was lined with all sorts of sewing machines. I decided not to go back to banking and law practice since I now had two children to take care of. The way we took care of our children in Nigeria was basically by proxy as the help did mostly everything, I even had to ask to hold the baby to nurse him. If they could produce breast milk, I guess they would also nurse the babies.

I had always had the spirit of enterprise and I had issues staying idle, so we put a sliding door in place of the door in the garage, since it was hardly used as a garage I converted it to a store for designer jeans and t shirts. It was the era of Karl Kani jeans and I had supplies from my Sister Ndy that I displayed in the garage.

Occasionally, young men would show up at the gates, seeking to buy the latest gear. This was before the cell phone era, so contacting you before coming was very rare. Life was going very well, Tony was doing very, very well with his real estate practice. He had a few very rich clients that entrusted him with picking out property and preparing their documents. It was generally a great life. He was very young for the maturity and professionalism that he exhibited. I remember once a client came to the door and said he was looking for Barrister Iromuanya, the secretary asked him to sit while he fetched the barrister. Tony was in the sewing section when he was informed that he had a client, he quickly made his way toward the law office as he put on his suit jacket. When he entered the room, the client was ushered into the office from the reception area and as he saw Tony's very young face, he informed him that he was not here to see him, but to see his father. It was hilarious, Tony asked if he was there to see Barrister Iromuanya. He answered the affirmative and he told him he was the one. That client ended up being one of his best customers. When he was not in the office, he was showing property or making clothes. He was so passionate about clothes and fashion, little wonder that some of our sons are also that way. Creativity, like I mentioned earlier, ran deep on both sides of the family. On a personal level, we were just admired by anybody that came in contact with us as a couple. We were re-writing history. Several of the people that had said negative things about us in the past were now Chinwe and Tony believers. Truly, at this point, we did not really care what people said and thought as occasionally news of negative comments would make its way to our ears. The stories were changing, they were no longer that Tony was not going to marry me since he has defied that, they were more or less about the fact that we must have gotten these babies from someone else while claiming that I gave birth to them.

They were entitled to their opinions.

I often wondered how possible it was for me to go through pregnancy and labor with no drama at all. That is where you have to truly understand that there is no one like God. When God decides to make an example of someone he does not seek consent from any one.

"But God hath chosen the foolish things of the world to confound the wise; and God hath chosen the weak things of the world to confound the things which are mighty." (1Corinthians1:27) What really can I say but, "Thank you, God!

My husband loved me more and more, and I watched my sons blossom, every trace of self-doubt that was still left in me, disappeared. You did not need anyone to tell you how much I rocked Tony's world. He allowed me the chance to be me. I knew who I was and a different man would have related with me differently by creating the impression that he was doing me a favor. That would have destroyed my self-confidence some more. My relationship with Tony was unique in the sense that even though there were the extraordinary circumstances they did not really come into play in the way that we related with each other; seriously, I wonder how it happened.

Because of the confidence I felt, I had no desire to prove anything to anybody anymore. When I felt the discrimination it no longer bothered me at all, I had a husband that told me daily that I was beautiful and I felt like people that did not treat me right, did not fully know my worth and they would change their minds if they did. I think it was at this point that the real Chi Chi was born.

I say this because people ask me if I always felt bold and strong, it was a journey and a process. I figured out after my marriage and the birth of the boys that really, there was no need to fit into anybody's box any more. There was a newfound confidence that when this man told me how incredible I was, he was not just saying it to get me in his bed, this handsome young man did not want to relate with me in secret, he wanted to shout to the roof tops that he was with me. And those sons of mine, they said it all to me, from the way Somto held tightly to me when I nursed him, to the way Chidera kissed me on my cheek and told me he loved me over and over; I would be a fool not to believe that I was worth something.

Still, those who were upset as the blessings grew were still there, they needed reasons to discredit this great testimony. Sometimes they would say my dad paid Tony huge amounts of money to marry me, that really hurt badly as it made me feel I was not worth any other person deciding to be with me. Looking back now, it is the plight of everyone living with disabilities in Nigeria in general, especially in Igbo land. This injustice is what I have dedicated my life to fighting. People who are living with disabilities, in the course of living life, can form great friendships. There are incredible human beings, like my Tony, that have the grace and heart to look beyond outward appearance and fall in love. Did Tony set out to love me from the first time he met me? My answer is a big no, even though he is the only one that can answer this question correctly, I do not think that was his intention.

I believe he gave the idea of friendship a chance and then began to fall in love with me as the friendship developed. From the developing friendship he discovered what I had to offer as a human being, instead of writing me off as flawed because of one thing that was different.

I decided to write this book to talk to a lot of the young ladies and gentlemen that are living with disabilities in Nigeria, for whom I present a face of hope and possibility, I cannot over-emphasize the need for friendship before marriage.

Before even bringing up the discussion of a relationship, I always ask the people that I mentor if they had good friends. Discrimination toward people that are different from us is deeply rooted in the area of marriage, it will take more that myself and the few role models we have in this area to make the change.

This runs even deeper amongst the educated ones, civilization has done very little to correct the thinking. It is still work in progress. We can begin to attempt to bring on this change when more people are willing to give people living with disabilities a chance. It takes a lot of planning and patience. Most of the young ladies get frustrated because they wish to be seen for who they are and when it does not happen they lose faith.

I understand these feelings and appreciate them, but I maintain that they need to change their mindset. We are not quite there as a people yet. You have to be patient.

For this reason, I will always sing Tony Iro's praises. He is such an incredible person, he never let all the discouragement get to him, there were people that asked him straight to his face if he was in clear understanding of what he was getting into. Now that we have gotten through the major hurdles, I can talk about these things. He told me of this guy that called him and pleaded with him not to marry me and he cautioned the guy never to speak to him again. He said the guy has now apologized and told him he was wrong.

When we share these stories, they no longer hurt me, I smile quietly. I asked him if he knew this was how it would play out. He said not quite, but that he was ready to stand by his decisions and the consequences. On my part, I have had my doubts about how far our bravery could carry us. Not because I did not have faith in what God would do, after all he has shown me enough miracles to believe he could finish it off. I was prepared for whatever the Lord decided to bring my way. I wondered as the seasons changed, especially in the days that followed our relocating to the United States, what would become of my family if I could not walk tomorrow. This reality made me plan daily, preparing my mind for anything. I did not take anything for granted. I woke up full of gratitude when I was able to take that first step with a bit of stiffness, but not much pain. At some points I had a whole lot of pain. So when others were startled at the imperfection, I was humbled at the possibilities.

I could spend a whole day talking about Tony and not stop, is he perfect? No. I can conveniently enumerate his flaws, just like he can mine, but that does not take away the fact that I could not have gotten this far without his help. The few years we spent in Nigeria as a couple before moving to the U.S. were sheer bliss, he showered me with all the love and affection a woman could wish for.

In Nigeria, I really did not do much in terms of work, but myself and the boys lacked for nothing. Every morning, I got up and dressed like I had somewhere very important to go to. No strand of hair was out of place, my nails beautifully manicured. I had two sons, but I never changed a soiled diaper, there were people whose duty it was to do that. Life was great, occasionally the thought of moving to America, would cross my mind and I would wave it aside and decide to consider that when the time came. I think somehow I was wishing and hoping it would never happen. One day something happened that made me change my mind. By this time, we had become born again and were members of the Redeemed Christian Church of God, a church with branches all over the world. Our pastor was our next door neighbor; it did not take him too long to recognize the gifts that we carried. Our pastor approached my husband and I with the possibility of heading a home fellowship. We accepted and the Lord was using us to do great things in the fellowship that we were heading. One day, the elders of the church came to our pastor's house and sent for us. They told me that they were on a mission, they had come to say some healing prayers on my behalf. I couldn't be healing other people when I needed healing myself.

It took me a little time to actually understand where they were coming from, remember I am not ordinarily aware that I have a disability. When I understood, I was a bit angry, but I did not let it show. I asked the Lord to give me the right answer. I told them that truly I did not see that I have any disability. That if the Lord was to come himself and ask me to choose one wish that I wanted to be granted, it would not be to correct my legs, I told them I understood clearly the purpose of my disability and I had no reason to query it. I went further to tell them I could bring more people to Christ than they could with their perfect legs, they apologized and left.

So our pastor was married to a very industrious woman, she would spend extensive time outside the country and return with lots of suitcases, I really cannot say if the items in the suitcases were gifts, personal effects, or merchandise as I always give people their personal space. So she returned home from a trip on this day. In the middle of the night, there was a lot of noise coming from the house next door. It was obvious there was a robbery going on. You could hear the robbers address the home owners and their very nervous responses at times. All other home owners in the area prayed, they did not know if their house would be next. My husband woke up and he shared with me a plan that he had in mind that would keep me and the family safe while he tackled the robbers should they attempt to enter our house. I was in shock and I knew that plan may not work exactly like he thought.

I could see the anxiety in his eyes and all I could do was to pray that it would never come to that for us. We nervously watched from our house, expecting the worst and soon the robbers left and there was unusual calmness in the neighborhood till it was obvious we were out of danger. From that day, I realized that we were not as safe as I thought.

This was not our first encounter with robbers and it was not my last. I remember less than two years prior, when I was pregnant with Chidera, my loving husband had taken me out on a date, it was at a restaurant located at a shopping mall, as we walked into this restaurant, there was a group of young men outside that politely ushered us in, we did not suspect anything out of the ordinary as we sat down and placed our order. Suddenly, I heard a loud voice shout, "shut up" to one of the other customers, I turned to Tony and told him this guy must be drunk. He was one of the young men that led us in. In a split second, the seemingly drunk guy pulled out a gun from his shirt and says, "Nobody should move!" He asked us to search ourselves and pull off any pieces of jewelry or money that we had on us and out it on the table. I was shaking like a leaf, remember I was about seven months pregnant. Tony pulled out his wallet and set it in front of us. He pulled me close and removes my engagement ring and puts it in his mouth, I was in shock! What if the robbers saw him? Soon they made the rounds collected what each customer laid out in front of them and then instructed us to go into the restroom, there were about thirty of us. To let us know they were serious, they planted a hot slap on the cheek of the restaurant owner and beat her with the butt of their guns, I could see her cheek begin to swell. Once we were settled in the restroom, they took all the money and fled without us knowing.

Meanwhile in the restroom, we were expecting the worst. Someone was crying, this was not really the time for tears as any noise could attract unnecessary attention. I just froze. I could feel some wetness on my clothes. I whispered to Tony that I think my water had broken. He was worried. Few minutes after that someone announced the robbers had left. We were in doubt at first, but one by one we started coming out of hiding. Once we got out, Tony examined me to investigate the source of the wetness on my clothes. We were relieved to learn that in that panic, I sat on an open bottle of Fanta. So this experience and the one that happened in our neighbor's house helped me make up my mind that I wanted something different for my family. My mind was finally made up. America here we come!

Once I made that decision, everything around me started to irritate me; I wished I was older and had a more balanced mindset like the one I have now. I would have done more research into the relocation. I would have approached my excitement and expectations with caution. I cannot say I was not warned. We had a friend of my sister's that fell in love with me and my young family. She was an American licensed pharmacist; she had lived in America for years, but returned to Nigeria to build an empire for herself in Lagos. She sent for me and asked me why I wanted to take my beautiful family to America, she said America would destroy my marriage and my life, she advised me not to go. I just refused to listen, nothing would have prepared me for the culture shock that I experienced when we relocated, but truth be told, I believe that the move was part of God's divine plan for me. You may want to know why? Psalm 37:23 says, "The steps of a good man are ordered by the Lord: and he delighted in his way." This was so true for my circumstances. Earlier in life when I had to go to boarding school and college away from home, I was challenging my muscles and I was gaining strength. With the way my life was structured as a married woman with means, I was gradually grinding to a halt. The Lord had a life of challenges planned out for me, one that would challenge all I knew as normal and make me stronger. Through very difficult and trying experiences, the Chi Chi Iro you know today emerged.

17

ALL IN EIGHT SUITCASES

*S*oon, we had an interview date from the embassy. We prepared for the interview, assembled the documents and the necessary fees. We were making an appointment for Tony, myself, two children and my cousin Ngozi. My relocating to America was contingent upon Ngozi coming with us; I would not make the mistake of traveling without Ngozi, it would be a disaster. I had no clue what to do with the boys, not because I lacked the physical strength, but because I had never taken care of the boys myself.

During the interview, the embassy staff agreed that he saw the need for Ngozi to travel with us, but could not justify that need.

He said we had to decide to go without her or not go. I quickly reminded myself of the reasons I wanted to leave, remember the insecure feeling from the robberies, better opportunity for the boys. So I quickly agreed to traveling without her, with the understanding that she would join us soon.

Once the visas were approved. It was time to start preparing to leave. Tony bought the tickets for Lagos to New York; it was scheduled for June, 1996. Now that the tickets had been paid for, it was time to prepare; we started disposing of all our possessions, we sold some and gave some away to family. We were allowed two suitcases each by the airlines, we intended not to exceed the eight suitcases we were allowed. Our biggest task was how to compress our lives into just eight suitcases. There were memories from years past, greeting cards, pictures and the children's memorabilia's that represented milestones, there were certificates and records for four people. There were diapers and formula and cereal; we needed a little of everything since we did not know how soon after arrival we could replenish supplies. We also needed to conserve funds. We had to decide what clothes to pack. As we started to put things together for the trip, I had mixed feelings but it was a bit too late for us to change our minds. As our possessions were sold one at a time and gifts were made, we moved to my big sister Ije's house, but not before selling five out of our six cars. The need to move to Ije's house arose because our home was no longer conducive for the boys. We would spend our last two weeks in Nigeria in her house then leave for the United States from there.

Sister Ije is a very kindhearted and reserved person. At that time, she was not married and had no kids; everyone in the family was afraid of her because she spoke very little, but was strict. She liked her things in order.

She had a beautiful apartment in Ikoyi that she opened up to us. I had my worries though. Having two active toddlers, Sister Ije's place was going to be a challenge, but the offer was a blessing. I want to mention that since the time, Sister Ije has gotten married, had two beautiful children, and has become extremely flexible. Oh! How circumstances change us. So we moved to her house and as the day approached we braced ourselves for the biggest journey of our lives. Nothing could have prepared me for how much our lives were going to change.

Remember, I had mentioned that between the two of us, Tony was the one more interested in learning how to care for the boys, this was way before the American lottery opportunity came to light. Tony had experience with how to care for babies when his younger brother, Leroy was born. When Leroy was born, he helped his mum take care of him. If you think  Tony is a great husband, he is an even a greater father. Watching Tony with our sons gives me goose pimples. Apart from the fact that they look like brothers, they have an excellent relationship. I have this picture that gives me so much joy, the picture of him leading our son to graduation.

In no time, June 20th came, we packed up our eight suitcases and two sons and headed for the airport. There were a lot of tears, as we were not sure if we were going to see our staff in this lifetime ever again. We were leaving what we knew to go to a very uncertain and unknown place. It was unknown and it was scary, but on the surface we acted like we had it figured out. Thank God for the mother care stroller (with bassinet combo that had a tray underneath) that Ndy had bought as a gift when Somto was born. I truly do not know how we juggled the boys and our carry-on luggage and walked the expanse of both airports; thinking back this was my arrogant days of not admitting my limits and requesting for wheelchair when I travelled. So I really cannot even imagine how I coped.

On the Flight, Somto slept a lot, he was just six months old and Chidera had just turned two years. The flight was long; Tony took care of the boys. Occasionally I breastfed Somto to soothe him. Soon we arrived in the US; there was great excitement as we disembarked. This would be the first time we saw Tony's mom who we called Lolo after marriage and two grandchildren.

As we approached the lobby at the airport we saw her; Lolo was as beautiful as I remembered, she had not aged a day since she left Nigeria several years ago, her beautiful light skin stood out as she launched excitedly toward us, heading for her grandkids. We all hugged her as she stepped back to look at us one at a time. Tony had just participated in a forty day fast and he was scrawny. I was exempt from the fast since I was nursing. She could not help but notice that he looked malnourished. She turned to me and asked me if I was not feeding my husband. Lolo had a way of finding humor in everything. I could not help laughing.

"Welcome to the America," she said as she helped us get out our eight pieces of luggage from the conveyor belt. Once we got the luggage, she led us to the car that was waiting. As we looked around us, I cannot say for sure what my husband was thinking, but I was thinking, "Is this America? It is filthy and hot. How in God's name am I supposed to survive here," as I tried to use mind control to block out the stench around me. Soon we got to the apartment in the Bronx, it looked like some of the apartments we saw on movies in Nigeria, there were rats everywhere and there were no air conditioners. I realized I had made the biggest mistake of my life, I didn't think, I would make it here. I wanted to go home. But hold on! The story just started.

That night it was time to debrief from the woman of leisure that I had always known myself to be and roll my sleeves up for the huge job called motherhood. Remember as a new wife, under the scrutiny of your mother in law, you were under observation 24/7. There were basic duties that your mother-in-law must see you perform. Nervously I went through the suitcases trying to figure out how Ngozi had done the packing while preparing the boys for their first shower by their mummy. Phew! I survived the shower part as I grabbed Somto's very heavy frame in my awkward fashion—under my arms as that was the only way I could balance my gait—as I made the journey to the bedroom to get him dressed. I remembered feeling a sense of panic as I recollected I had asked Ngozi to remove the towels she had packed for the trip because they made the box heavier. I presumed there would be plenty of fresh clean towels in America.

Using one hand to restrain Somto, I frantically used the other hand to search for a towel while praying Som did not pee all over the place. I found one and breathed a sigh of relief as I muttered, 'God bless Ngozi' under my breath. Getting the pull ups on Chidera as I dressed him up that night was not much of a problem, but getting the diaper on Somto, a chubby active six-month old, was a little bit of a challenge. I managed to align the Velcro, but it looked a little lop sided, I softly called out to Tony. He was catching up with his mum, I did not want her to believe I was not equipped for the task ahead. He came promptly and I used sign to tell him that I needed help with the diaper. He let out a big laugh and said, "Na wah! Alarm go blow you o! How are you going to survive with two children and no maid?" There was something about the way he reacted to the events of that evening that made me angry yet challenged me. Why was he talking so loud? Did he want to expose my weaknesses in front of his mum? As he adjusted that diaper, I observed what he was doing, resolving never to ask for this type of help again. That night, Chichi the house help and Chichi the mother was born. As we settled down to sleep in the hot New York night, I noticed a big fat rat run across the room as I sighed and fought back tears. I regretted making this trip with my sons that had never experienced lack. This was not my scene; I would give anything to go back home. But which home? There was no home. That home had been dismantled, it was time to try to make sense of this new home, I thought to myself as I prayed for sleep to overpower me. Tony was snoring beside me, he was tired and so were our little princes. I was still a bit of upset at Tony for handling the diaper incident the way he did, I had never been this upset with him. I prayed this relocation would not chip away the foundation of our love. Soon sleep came and I forgot the events of the day. In my mind, I was having a nightmare that I would soon wake up from. Something happened the next morning that let me know it was the other way round.

I got up real early and started to give the boys a bath and get them ready. I had Somto on the bed and looked away for a moment, by the time, I turned to him, he was eating something and he was also bleeding. I panicked, reached into his mouth and retrieved a piece of glass as I called out to Tony. I was not sure how much of the glass he had swallowed already and we did not know what to do. Tony called out to his mum and she suggested we should call the ambulance. An ambulance was called and we headed out to the emergency room. On getting to the emergency room, the attending physician was a Nigerian doctor who had the same last name, Iromuanya. He found it fascinating as he came out to meet the parents of the glass crushing youngster. It happened that he was also from Umuahia..

After the usual pleasantries he reassured us that Somto was going to be okay. What an experience! When you add it to every other thing going on in our lives, there were no words to describe the entire experience. As if that was not enough, my sister, Ndy, had asked me to get her something from a store in Manhattan. Lolo had insisted I go with her, we went partially by bus and walked the rest of the way, by the time, I came home, I had blisters all over my feet. I was done with pretending I was coping with this harsh life. I needed a way out. How did people survive this life? This was torture, there was no escape. Why did I think this was a better life? I really wanted to go home. It was around this time that my sister, Ihuoma, invited us to come visit her in Dallas, we took a few of our belongings, and made the trip to Dallas. Dallas it was a different world. They lived in a bungalow in a small city called The Colony; it was not a big house, but it was like a castle compared to the apartment we were coming from in Bronx. When it was time to go home, I was not ready to go. The fantastic part of that was that she also had four sons and the cousins enjoyed being together.

Tony was ready to go back to New York. I had informed earlier him that we were not ready to go with him and that he should please pack our belongings and send back for us. I knew that there was no way he would go back and leave us in Dallas.

While we were with my sister the household duties increased; I had to take care of the boys as well as her own kids when she was out. I did not mind, since anything was better than the apartment in Bronx.

Later in the month, Tony returned with our belongings, we had rented a small bungalow in the same area that my sister lived in Texas. As Tony was leaving New York he had asked Lolo if we could have a small radio that she owned and she said yes. We moved into the house not owning much except that small radio. The only seat in the house was the brick in front of the fire place. Tony had gone to the dollar store nearby to buy a broom, some pots, and dishes. I was now an expert at caring for the boys. I took time to get them ready daily. Thankfully, we had some good quality clothes we brought so they still looked fairly decent. One day at a garage sale, Tony bought a water bed and a blue and silver retro chair. Those remained the only pieces of furniture for a long time.

Daily, I would clean the almost empty apartment and cook after taking care of the boys. In no time, Tony got his first job and then his second. We were struggling to make ends meet. We had quickly gone through our reserve. Then he added a third job, we now saw very little of him, leaving me to be the primary care giver for the boys. In my days in Port Harcourt I had had an accident with my Honda Civic that made me very afraid to drive. So living this remote suburb, there were very limited job choices for someone that did not drive. Tony had bought a car from the auction and it gave him the flexibility to shuttle between jobs. When he came home, he was tired, irritable ,and sometimes angry; he knew we would have had better options in New York. We could have taken the New York Bar and start practicing, but there was no way I was going to go back to New York. I would not survive there. For now, we were going to live beneath our level while praying and trusting God. I could tell our once perfect lives were falling apart. I was homebound with two little boys and there was nowhere to go. The more frustrating my situation became the more I put my energy into the boys and the home.

I mastered the art of motherhood and homemaking, I discovered it was something that I was made for. I had acquired the skills to perform these tasks excellently, it made other women appear inadequate. As I got better with these things I stopped recognizing who I was, there was a huge conflict going on inside of me. America was recreating me; it was recreating us. I was too afraid to think of who I would become when the job was done. Whenever Tony was off work, he made an effort to be the father and husband that we knew, but I could see in his eyes, the same conflict and uncertainty that I felt.

This was not what we had in mind when we decided to relocate. It was not working out. As each of us nursed our fears and worries, there were stories of other professionals that had migrated under the DVI program and when things did not work out for them, they took their lives. They were moved to do that because America was not working out and the home they left behind was no longer the home they felt like returning to. They were people in the same situation that we found ourselves, the only difference was that we loved each other and had two children that we had no intention of abandoning by taking our own lives.

One day, there was a knock on the door. I was battling a really bad cold and feeling sorry for myself with Ama and Somto running around the empty house. I made it to the door and there was this beautiful, kind-looking white lady, she introduced herself as Angel. Angel was my angel that day, she took one look at me and ran to the grocery store to fetch some fruits and cold medication, this was the first act of kindness I had received from anyone other than Tonkin a long time. Angel was a member of the Church of Christ; we became friends and she started taking us to their church and home bible meetings. Angel reintroduced me to the outside world, I felt alive again, she had a young son, Drew, who was Chidera's age, so the friendship was perfect for me and my sons. Strange that I reconnected with Angel some weeks ago through Facebook. It was such joy recounting all the memories from our early days in the United States. The relocation was a real tough journey that only the Lord could have brought us through.

18

LIGHT AT THE END OF THE TUNNEL

One day we found out about an organization that would help us with our transition properly. They looked at our lives at that time and made certain recommendations, this was at a time that most good jobs required computer knowledge, they linked Tony up with a good program, advised us to move to an apartment to avoid the extra expenses that came with living in a house. The apartment they recommended was on a bus route which meant either of us could get to work without driving, they also helped us with basic needs, including help with childcare. The new life came with mixed feelings, so much damage had already happened to my self-esteem. On the positive side, I had increased physical strength and more control of my muscles especially the muscles in my hand which had gained better coordination from all I had been forced to do for my family. To be honest the increased strength was something I did not pay much attention to, nor did I appreciate it at the time. I was too focused on regrets and resentment, I had no understanding of the changes that were happening behind the scene. I was an ungrateful spoiled brat, but because of the promise that God had made to me, he kept smiling at me and putting things in place.

The pain in my heart concerning where I found myself was enormous.

Sometimes I wondered how someone with the potential and background that I had ended up where I was. Throughout this time, I avoided the mirror because I did not recognize the image of the person in the mirror anymore. Any idea of my self-worth just flew out of the window. I guess I was not much of a friend and companion to my husband at this time also. I have always said that you really cannot give to someone else what you do not possess. I do not know why I sank my energy in housework and motherhood, I guess those areas were where I felt more secure building or maybe a greater power was preparing me for the task ahead.

On Sundays, Angel, her husband Matt, and Drew would come get me and the boys to go to church. I was getting irritated at everything by this time. The problem with Angel's church was they talked to me like I knew nothing about God. They were of the opinion that only members of their church had a relationship with God. I was frozen in my mind. I did not want to say anything to anybody, I did not want to do anything. I was homesick. I desired to turn back the clock and get my old life back. I did not have the spiritual maturity at this time to do that. Unlike before I came to the United States, I had so much going for me, I knew who I was.

One day Tony had a conversation with me. He told me that he wanted us to work together and figure out a way to get out of our present predicament, he said if we did not do that, we ran the risk of compounding the problems. He said part of the things we needed to consider was not having any more children so we could get our lives sorted out. I heard him alright, but I just did not have a clue what he wanted me to do. This same Tony was the one that told me earlier that he had figured out why people that were having financial challenges had a lot of children, he said the reason was that when everything failed they at least had the companionship of each other. We really fit into that group, we were financially challenged but we had each other.

I had started work at a company where I took calls. Tony had worked in the same company during his three job era so he gave me the lead. I had a friend living in our apartment complex that worked at the same place too. Things were beginning to look up a bit, or so I thought. God had other plans as you will find out soon. Moving to the apartment we came into contact with some other Nigerians, we had not met any Nigerians apart from my sister, her family, and her friends. When we lived in the Colony, my sister had several friends, but she was my older sister and I felt it would be better to keep away from her friends. I did not want to steal any one's friends, moreover, I was searching for myself.

One day this cab driver came to drop off a guest at our miserable house in the Colony, it so happened, he was Nigerian and he had been in America for a long time. As was customary for us, once I knew he was Nigerian, I asked him in and offered him a drink. I informed him that my husband was due home soon. As he sipped his drink, he curiously asked what we were doing in a dead place like the Colony? He observed our sons open and close the refrigerator like they were hoping Jesus would repeat his miracle of "fish multiplication to feed 5,000"; they were not having much success. In the meantime, this guy took everything in without saying a word. Soon Tony returned and I did the introductions, then he asked Tony if we had a grocery store nearby, Tony said yes. He told Tony he had a young son just like Chidera and that he had promised his baby mama he was going to buy grocery for the son, but that he did not know what to buy so he needed Tony's help buying food that a child the same age as our son would like. Tony was happy to be of service and took him to the neighborhood grocery store and they shopped endlessly, when they returned to the house he asked Tony to help him bring in all the groceries and that it was for our boys. We were in tears, we had never seen such kindness. That was how we made our first friend. His name was Dennis. Dennis was not just a friend, he was like an older brother. He took time to educate us on how to keep our heads afloat in a place like Dallas, soon one good turn deserved another as Tony told Dennis how to get a job in the Customer Service firm where I was now working. So if I found a way to work, I was guaranteed to have a ride back. Dennis would always bring me back after work. One remarkable thing about Nigerians that relocated to the United States at the time, was they were determined to succeed...Except me, I was still home sick.I just wanted to go back home.

There was something special about this apartment we moved to that gave me some sort of control in my life, I think it was the fact that it was clean and new and most things were set out in a more organized fashion than the house in the Colony. One of the things that tickled my fancy was the fact that it had a microwave, it was incredible that a microwave could excite me that much. It kind of illustrates how low I had sunken, since I owned my first microwave in my little corner at Imo State University, several decades earlier, but with the poverty that we had experienced recently, a microwave was novelty.

The apartment had a living room and dining room with a kitchen off the living room. It was a brand new apartment on Rosemead road in Carrollton. The agency that was offering their assistance had let us have a striped cream and red sofa. We even had a black coffee table and side stool with lamps. My sister Ihuoma had just cleared out the furniture from my father's house and she gave us a black and white dining set with four chairs and a complete bedroom set which we put in the master bedroom. Things were beginning to look better. One day on his way back from work, Tony brought home a vacuum cleaner and a television, my goodness! That was the happiest day of my life. It meant I could watch shows like Marsh and I Love Lucy when I did not have any housework to do and the boys were in bed. Everything was looking promising and would have remained so if I had listened to Tony and not let the next thing happen.

In those days, without having medical insurance, family planning was something that only the elite could afford. In my understanding it was more affordable to get pregnant and stop buying tampons for nine months than to seek family planning. So I woke up one day and realized the unthinkable had happened. I knew my body so well there was really no need to run a pregnancy test. I was ninety-nine percent sure I was pregnant; the problem was that, this was not part of my husband's plans. Things were just starting to look up for us. I was very nervous, unlike the other times that I was pregnant and my husband was over the moon with joy. I knew this would not be the case, he had told me that if I wanted us to fall right back into poverty that another child would do just that.

I was wondering how I was going to conceal this as long as possible so that I could postponed the inevitable. I knew I could pull it off for a couple of months going by my previous pregnancies. I hardly looked pregnant till I had the baby, the one thing I was going to do was just act tough. Go to work, come back. Take care of the boys, cook, clean, and take the laundry downstairs to the laundry room and wash without complaint. I must try my best never to ask for help. I tried to do all this for months and pulled it off successfully, sometimes Tony would ask me why he had not noticed me have my period and I would say, "It just passed." You know how we women look to other women for support, there was no way I could go through this very tough times without having support so I confided in our friend Maureen, but made her promise she would not tell anyone not even her husband Festus, who was Tony's very close friend at the time. I know she will crack up when she reads this and remembers this plot, she was sort of concerned how I was going to keep all this a secret. I just told her I would try my best. Maureen was younger than I was, but she brought her heart to America and irritated me often by saying she never wanted to go back to Nigeria. Maureen was also very frugal, I guess she had seen the memo on coming to America and I had not. Looking back, I needed to be more like Maureen.

This was during the time of analog phones and part of our living the American dream was the ability to afford two handsets from Target or Walmart for about ten dollars. The bad thing about having two phones in different rooms was, you could be on one handset and someone could pick the other one in the other room and listen to the entire conversation. We had one handset on the ledge that separated the living room from the kitchen and the breakfast nook with the black and white dining set. The other handset was in the bedroom. After a long day, finally relieved I was home alone with the boys and could share my secret with my friend, I got on the phone with Maureen. We were gladly taking about our little secret, unknown to both of us, Tony had come in and wanted to use the phone, he heard us talking and decided to listen some more. He could not believe his ears. I was pregnant and he did not know about it. I guess he did not know how to react, he knew that we were doing a dangerous tango that sounded like "quick quick slow slow" we were taking several steps forward and plenty backwards. Bang! Bang! Poof! went whatever progress we made. Knowing Tony, he had to calm himself to handle this in a very mature manner. He entered the bedroom, once I saw him I was startled since I did not have prior knowledge that another adult was in the apartment. I guess at that time I did not think he heard our conversation. I quickly ended the conversation with Maureen. Once I was off the phone, he calmly said, "So you are pregnant? Why did you not tell me?" I froze, I did not know how to take the question. I told him I was afraid, since he had previously told me that if I wanted us to be in perpetual poverty in America, the fastest way was to have another child. He held me and told me that even though he had said that there was really nothing we could do once the pregnancy happened. I could see he had a worried look that he was trying so hard to conceal. I was relieved that my secret was out. I was also happy that there was a possibility we would be having a girl. I wanted a girl so bad. Focusing on pregnancy and not appreciating the reality of the problem that we faced ahead was an issue. There was the matter of prenatal care. There was another issue as the pregnancy progressed. I was having a continuous period. Yes, I knew I was pregnant, but it was not adding up why was I having this endless period. Could this pregnancy be my imagination. Do not forget that I had neither seen a doctor nor had a test done. My belief in the pregnancy was due to my knowledge of my body. This worry made me desire this pregnancy more than anything. At this time Maureen herself had become pregnant with her first child and I had also met some other friends. Amaechi and Adanna. Adanna is a medical doctor, she has a thriving practice now. Our families knew each other; she knew me from Nigeria too. Her husband Amaechi was a friend of mine from the University, he was also a lawyer. I was quite friendly with Amaechi, we had been members of the Dollar Club in Imo State University and had formed a good bond over a very popular song by an artist called Bunny Mark that was called "My Sweetie, My Sugar." I had no idea Amaechi was in Dallas, till one day he ran into Tony and during introduction he realized I was Tony's wife. We were so excited to reconnect. Amaechi promised to bring his wife Adanna to meet me and he kept his promise over that weekend. Adanna was also pregnant, mine was a little more advanced than hers. Adanna and I became instant sisters, she had the sort of personality that made me want to dig deep to uncover who I was and who I ought to be. There was something unique about my relationship with Adanna that made me find my path. She believed in me and my counsel. My word was gospel to Adanna, she seemed blinded to the fact that I was not living up to the image that she knew. To this day Adanna challenges me in the way she views others.

She is always telling others I was a positive influence in her life, but she did not realize what she did for me. I was older than she was by a few years, yet she made me feel that my opinion mattered, she also knew me and my accomplishments before I came to America. I have never tried to put this period in words, to explain to my good friend the role she played in helping me find who I was meant to be.

Between my two pregnant friends who were almost five months pregnant, they convinced me that it was time to see the doctor. They let me know that if you were pregnant that the government would grant you Medicare during the pregnancy. So that information saved the day. At five months I made my first appointment with a gynecologist and braced myself for the worst. I had expected her to tell me that I was pregnant. On the day of my first appointment she ran my first pregnancy test and confirmed that my suspicions were right, I was pregnant alright, but her jaw dropped when she asked me the last time I saw my period, I said I had become pregnant five months earlier but then I saw a period every day despite my belief that I was pregnant. She asked me to get on her table so that she could use her fingers and tape to measure the fundal heights and try to estimate the age of my pregnancy. If you remember from my other pregnancies I was one of those women that you could not measure their pregnancy that way, since once I laid down the pregnancy disappeared to my back. The doctor was sweating, in her opinion something was not adding up here. She quickly abandoned that route and said she would suggest a sonogram. She decided to investigate a little further into my bleeding complaint, she decided to give me a vaginal examination, as soon she did that, she found the culprit, she informed me that the placenta was sitting quite low and that the examination could make it better or worse. After that examination, I experienced a miracle. That was the last day I had any form of bleeding till the baby was born. God just loves me and I know it.

I was still very homesick and wanted so much to go back home. With a new baby on the way, I needed help. I was really lonely even though I had made more friends. I missed my family.

Once Tony left for work, I got on the phone and called Nigeria. International calls were very exorbitant at the time, but I did not care. I would get on the phone with my mum and tell her the importance of getting Ngozi here as soon as possible. They had assisted her in applying to the United States Embassy, but each time she was refused visa. This was very unusual knowing the sort of influence my parents had.

In my understanding of things now, all that was part of God's grand plan. He was not punishing me, he was preparing me for the task ahead. Knowing my personality, if anyone had made the mistake of telling me that, I would have had their head for dinner.

While waiting for Ngozi to come and relieve me, I needed to reason things out. Due to the pregnancy and the extended bleeding, I had to stop work again. My husband, in search of answers, was now turning to prayer. Redeemed had not really started at this time, but he had met some Nigerians at his part time job at Toyota of Richardson. They attended a small church group which was a branch of the then Zoe Ministries. We had also, as a family, started attending Covenant Church, throughout this time I did not forget my Christian faith, but I had lost hope.

I am naturally a questioner and that has always been the way I related to God. I had private moments because I was alone most times and instead of the day dreams that I filled my life with earlier, I spent time asking a lot of questions and trying to make sense of it all. I got answers I did not like most times and I could not figure out the relevance of the things that I was going through.

As I write this I cannot help but marvel at God's faithfulness, it hurt him to see me in that much pain, but he who knew the end from the beginning knew that he would take me through this process to make me stronger.

One day my whole mindset switched. I was in personal turmoil, I constantly asked God why he answered our prayers when we were first born again in Nigeria but not since we moved to America. The answers he gave me blew my mind. He first asked if I thought he was going to answer instantly to my demands forever? He said at that time he answered us swiftly that we were new relationships, he was trying to get our attention. He said, "Now you know me, you have to build your trust and faith. Will I answer? Yes! But in my time." I was learning. He said, "whatever situation that comes your way, know that I will never desert you, not forsake you. No matter how bad things get I will make a way for you. In your wildest dream, did you think you would have gotten here?" That encounter was humbling. I had a shift in my thinking. This was the beginning of a new way of reasoning for me. Throughout the wretchedness and hopelessness of this period, a new Chinwe was emerging, it was a journey that taught me how to be alone; I was changing. Finally, I was getting it.

There have been times I retreated to this alone place with God to gather strength for the road ahead and sometimes he would allow me time to mingle and roam free having his promises with me and knowing that no matter how hard things get He would see me through. I have written stories upon stories as I further reason this journey of mine out. This was the moment where it began to come clear to me. Many have asked me before if I have always been strong? My answer is "No." I am as weak and vulnerable as every other woman, but I know one answer to that question and it is found in Psalm121: 1 and 2, "I lift up my eyes to the hills. From where does my help come from? My help comes from the Lord. The maker of heaven and earth." What a blessing it was to come to this realization.

I will like you to also find peace in some bible verses. My favorites of all time:

"For as the heavens are higher than the earth, so are my ways higher than your ways, and my thoughts than your thoughts."

(Isiah 55:9)

"God knows exactly his reasons for everything. Trust in Lord with all your heart; Lean not on your own understanding. In all things acknowledge his ways."

(Proverbs 3-5)

As I journeyed, these verses have kept me focused and strong. My friends noticed a sudden transformation, the new Chi Chi had emerged, positive and full of promise.

19

IKECHI-BY GOD'S STRENGTH!

rying so hard to walk in my new path as one who was going to trust God no matter what, my reality presented more and more issues arising. The apartment we lived in was a two-bedroom apartment. Tony was doing quite well career wise, unlike the customer service that most Nigerians had, he was now working with EDS.

He was now a salaried man working in a telecommunications company due to the computer training he acquired. There was a new problem. The rules for occupancy was two people to a room in Texas, if we were expecting a baby we had to move to a three bedroom apartment. Most available three-bedroom housing was bungalows. After our harrowing experience at the Colony we were very opposed to living in a home, so we searched really hard and found this three-bedroom townhome in a place called Richardson, Texas.

For us, it meant we could enjoy a building on two floors, there was the fairly large living room downstairs with a dining room and kitchen. We had a patio behind the kitchen door which meant the boys could ride their bikes.

The boys, oh yes, I have not spoken about them for some time. Chidera had now sort of sobered down, he was kind of shy and always wanting to follow rules, which is typical of the way first born kids are raised in Africa. From a very early age they learn responsibility. They start early to sacrifice for their younger siblings. On the contrary, Somto was growing more confident. I nursed Somto up until the time that I found out I was pregnant. Somto loved his food, I had no clue how to wean him off the breast milk.

I had to send him to our friend Ngozi for three days in order to wean him off. Somto was big and he used his big frame to intimidate Chidera at times.

Chidera was the perfect child while Somto was strong-willed from childhood. I would lay the rules out and Chidera would follow, but Somto would always find a way to defy my authority. Sometimes this child would test my patience and the only way I would not beat him blue and black was to remember the things my mom used to advise other mothers who told her they had a child that tried their patience. She would tell them that she had been to different markets, but she had never seen a market that offered a stubborn child for sale and at other times she would just say this one liner, "Onye atufule." A person can change at any time, do not discard without giving them a chance." These two sayings from Mama kept me going through out the times that Somto tried my patience. This was where we were at the time we moved to the town home in Richardson.

It was spacious and a decorator's dream. I was a little relaxed so I did not waste time resurrecting my decorating skills. Even though we moved with the furniture from Carrollton, the way I put it together was unique.

I had mastered how to cook some delicious dishes at this time. A lot of them were poor man's improvised versions of some African dishes like making the popular onugbu soup with oatmeal instead of fresh coco yams. There were very few stores that sold African goods at that time. For fufu powder we used baking flour and mashed potatoes. Such a wonder how we escaped obesity considering the bad reputation that most foods that are white have now, most of my friends had children and did not work so it was not unusual to see a lot of mothers and their children gather at our home in Richardson.

I had one favorite dish, potato casserole with chicken. To make it you needed just a bag of Russet potatoes and a pack of chicken quarters and any vegetables of your choice. My favorites then were carrots, cucumbers, and green peppers. First I spent time peeling the potatoes, then I cut them in cubes then soaked them in cold water while I skinned the chicken quarters and cut them in small pieces too. I would season the chicken and add in the potatoes and when the potatoes were tender I would add in the veggies. Voila! You had a pot of wholesome cooking for under ten dollars.

There was one problem with our new townhome. There were roaches everywhere. Someone once said that if they did not know I was a clean freak, they would have said it was dirt that attracted the roaches. The roaches had no respect for anything, the more I cleaned the more they appeared. I did not know what to do about them, it was as if they found a way to come from the other apartments and caused me great distress.

Sometimes when Tony saw how much they upset me, he would go to Home Depot and buy bug sprays. . He would open all the cabinets and move the food out and then set it off while we left home for the day. Upon our return, we would see carcass of dead roaches, we would rejoice at our conquest.

In the days that followed, they would re-appear. We signed a one-year lease, we could not just get up and leave. Several times we complained to the management and they would send fumigators, who would ask us to vacate for the day and return in the evening, still the roaches were a menace.

I will never forget one incident that happened. I was busy cooking up a storm and some mothers had gathered to eat. I was getting the food ready when a roach fell into the pot. If I had been the only one that saw it? I would have scooped that section of the food out and we would have eaten it without much problem, since I noticed it as soon as it fell in, but one of the other ladies saw it and started screaming. I was so embarrassed. We had to throw the entire pot of food out.

Life can take us through different terrain. Anyway this chapter is not about the roaches and the trouble they caused us, it is a chapter to introduce number three, Ikechi. I wanted a girl so badly, but somehow I knew that was not going to happen. I wanted to confirm the sex of the baby, so I decided to have a sonogram. The sonogram confirmed it was another boy, initially I was a little bit disappointed, but I talked to myself as usual. I asked myself if I even believed I would have any children with my disabilities and that the right attitude was an attitude of ingratitude. If there was ingratitude it disappeared as the date of Ikechi's birth played out.

As usual, it was the same story, there was the risk of premature delivery as was my pattern. Doctors once more had confirmed that it was a boy. They were managing the situation and were doing their best to get me to thirty-six weeks,

Things were going very well. Chidera was just four at the time. He woke up on the morning of that day and told his dad that he dreamt that there was a rope around the neck of the baby I was carrying in my stomach and that the baby died and we had to call the police. We were kind of worried since it was very unusual for a four-year-old to recall a dream so vividly. I had my weekly checkup that day and Tony was working. I had arranged for my sister-in-law, Ijeoma, to take me to the hospital. Ijeoma drove me to the doctor's. The doctor asked me to lie down and measured me over and over, while trying to listen to the baby's heart. She looked very concerned. She kept asking me if I knew when I got pregnant, I told her not to bother with the measurements because I knew they would not be accurate. She decided to send me to do a sonogram requesting to have the results immediately. I remember waiting to see the doctor after the test. I was thirsty and I asked the nurse if she could give me a glass of water and she said it may not be advisable and that the doctor was coming to talk to me. I was not bothered by what she said. I knew deep in my heart I was not in any kind of danger.

A few minutes later, the doctor emerged, she asked me if I felt the baby move the entire day. I thought for a moment and said not much. She said she was worried about the baby's progress, she said she knew the baby was alive at the time of the sonogram, but nothing was making sense about the pregnancy. I tried to explain to this doctor, her name was Dr. McClintock, that nothing ever made sense about me or my life, including my pregnancies, she just looked at me like I was crazy. Remember this was my first pregnancy in the United States and there were no medical records to go by. So she told me what she would recommend.

She asked me to make arrangements to meet her in the hospital, that the baby would be delivered in a few hours and that she would be waiting for me. She told me to prepare my mind for the worst. Immediately I remembered little Chidera's dream from that morning and I was almost giving in to the spirit of fear when I encouraged myself with God's promise to me concerning my pregnancies and delivery.

I placed a call to my husband, letting him know all the doctor had said and told him I was heading to Presbyterian Hospital in Plano and that he should take the boys to his mom and meet me there. I also asked him to bring my packed luggage for labor. The pregnancy was just thirty-four weeks along. My sister-in-law dropped me off by the front desk of the hospital. I told them I was going into labor and delivery and as usual they asked me what for since I did not look pregnant. I informed them I was pregnant, gave them the doctor's name and they took me up. Dr. McClintock had called ahead and let them know I was coming. Once I was shown to a room, I called home and when Tony did not answer, I knew he was already headed to his mum's. I called her house and she said they were on their way there. I told her to have him call me once he arrived and I gave her my room number. Several minutes later he called back and just before he said, "I know you are a Hebrew woman, please do not have the baby before I get there." I told him I was not sure the Hebrew woman powers would happen this time.

While I was on the phone with him, the nurses got things ready. They started the infusion that was supposed to get things ready. According to their calculations, it would be a few hours before we would see any signs of action. I informed her I had had two precipitated labors and she looked at me like she was going to say "yeah right." Once she left the room, I placed  a call to my sister, Ihuoma, and we talked about my experiences. She is a nurse and I wanted to get her opinion. While on the phone, I felt like the baby was in between my legs. I told my sister to stay on the phone because I needed to call the nurse, she asked me why and I told her I thought the baby was here. She just laughed at me and said it was impossible. I pressed the help button, nurse comes in and I informed her that I thought the baby was here. I was in between the sheets; my sister was still on the phone. About fifteen minutes after we started the process, she pulled down the sheets to have a look, what she saw shocked her. The baby had crowned! She could see the head and all the curly black hair. She held my legs apart with one hand, panicking as she screamed, "I NEED HELP!" This time she pressed the help button herself. Several nurses came running in. There was a problem, the neonatal intensive care unit was supposed to be there, they were expecting a premature baby. The baby was out before my doctor made it to the room. I still had my makeup and dangling earrings on!.

Thirty minutes later, my husband walked into my room, dragging my suitcase behind him, he stopped for a moment to take in what he was seeing. I was on the bed holding our third son and smiling. He said, "Why did you have to have the baby before I got here? I have never missed a delivery. This is so not fair!" I told him the one thing that should matter to him now was the fact that both his son and I were alive and well and he relaxed. With our two other children, we had picked out their names before they were born. This one came way too early. We did not have a name yet. Considering everything that happened that day, no name would work better than Ikechi, meaning, by God's strength. Only God could have done this. Several minutes later, Dr. McClintock came in and congratulated us and admitted that I had warned her about how fast my labor was, but this was the fastest she had ever seen in her entire medical career.

She apologized for making me have the baby so early, she said now that the baby was out, there was absolutely nothing wrong with him and that he did not even need to go to the incubator. I told her that I appreciated the fact that she took proactive steps. Who knows what would have happened if we waited. Ikechi made his grand entrance on April 3rd. He was slightly less than what his brothers weighed at birth as he weighed only seven pounds eleven ounces. God was so good to us!

Later that evening, Tony went to get the other boys from his mother's place and before they went home, he brought them to see their baby brother. I was not really prepared for this baby. Since this was my first baby in the United States, I needed everything. My sister had given me a baby shower, I got a few gifts, but I still needed a few more things. He was born on Friday and by Sunday, we were ready to head back home. Tony came with the boys and a car seat, we set the new baby in the seat of our Honda Accord and left. We made a brief stop at Target, picked a few items, and continued.

Life in those days was very challenging, I had a few friends like I mentioned, but everyone was busy with their lives and family and I was not one to ask for help, truly I did not trust anyone to do the things I was doing to my standard.

Looking back now, I have always been concerned about attracting the wrong attention to my family. I did not want anyone to feel sorry for my husband for having a wife living with disabilities, so I mastered the art of survival and perfected it. To the point that so many times, I went out of my way to offer assistance to other women that were visibly more physically endowed than I was. Support was something that was nonexistent in my life at that time. Unlike the previous pregnancies, where I had Sister Lizzy, this time we were by ourselves. The first thing I had to figure out was how this was going to work. The next morning, Tony left for work while we were still sleeping. I was praying the older boys would sleep longer as I assembled the baby's supplies. I unpacked the sterilizing pot. It was a stainless steel pot with a little hole on top to let out the steam, it had a plastic divider on the inside that had provisions for different size bottles, nipples, and covers. I really wanted an electric sterilizer like the mother care brand I used in Lagos, but could not find one in the stores. The only problem with this steam one and the hole on the cover was the roaches, so once the bottles were sterilized and cool, I wrapped the entire pot with plastic wrap.

I used the same technique to secure the crib and bassinet. Whenever my baby was sleeping I would wrap him up with netting like the one we used to ward off mosquitoes but this time with the hope of keeping the roaches at bay. The roaches were out with a vengeance. If there was anything I hated about this apartment it was the roaches. While all three kids were sleeping, I went over my strategies. I took my shower, pulled out the baby bath bucket and filled it with hot water, I also fetched the tray that had all the baby supplies, everything was so new and cute. I got the Winnie the Pooh hooded towel out and set it on the bed. I pulled back the mosquito net and got our baby son out for his first bath. There was something so special about that first bath at home. Apart from the fact that it was very therapeutic for the baby, it gives a mother a better opportunity to appreciate her bundle of joy. Slowly and meticulously, I gave baby Kechi his first bath, massaging every part of his body, the way I observed Lizzy do, then after that I wrapped him up in the hooded towel and set him in the bed, I reached for the baby lotion and oil and greased him from his head to his feet, stretching his arms and legs like I knew to do. Finally, I dressed him up in his onesie and bib then latched him unto my waiting nipples. As he fed, I counted my blessings, number three was so cute! Another blessing from God. Who am I, Lord, that you are mindful of me. He fed for some time as I switched him from one breast to the other till I noticed he was no longer suckling. He was sleeping. I propped him up to burp him and then once he let out a burp like a drunken sailor, I laid him in his crib and covered him with the netting.

I went to wake Chidera and Somto, put them in the shower at the same time, dressed them up, and took them down for breakfast. This was going to be our daily routine in that order. Once the older boys were fed, I sat down to watch a little television. This was our first day home. I was a bit tired and I dozed off while watching T.V. I woke up some time later, there was an uneasy quietness in the house, that is for a house with two toddlers and a baby. I rushed up the stairs in a state of panic, everything seemed normal till I got to the babies room that doubled as the guest room, the older boys had heard my footsteps and disappeared, on the floor was my baby that I had just finished bathing and feeding. He was stark naked. The entire room and furniture was covered in white talcum powder. The baby was covered in powder too. When the boys heard my footsteps they hid. These two rascals had taken out the pacifier from the complimentary baby bag I brought home from the hospital and plugged the baby's little mouth. So there was a powder covered baby on the carpet sucking away at the pacifier, wide eyed. I fell to the floor crying as I picked up the baby, inspected him for any sign of injury, pulled out the pacifier and tried to smell his breath to see if he had ingested any chemicals. I cleaned him up, held him close till he slept again, then took him to my bed while I cleaned the nursery and changed his sheets. While doing these things, I was calming myself because if I did not calm down, I would kill those two rug rats.

Most mothers would admit that what makes us cry in situations like this is just the hopelessness of the situation. Will this be my life? How do I begin to clean this colossal mess? I remember Mama's wise words, "The eyes are cowards." As I bent down and picked the almost empty container of baby powder, I fetched a bucket of water and towel and started wiping down all the surfaces. Finally, as I ran the vacuum over the floor, I said to myself, "I can do this!" By the time I finished, I was calm. I did not beat Chidera and Somto that day. I cleaned them up, fed them, and gave them a little lecture. Soon, Daddy was back, but I did not bother telling him the story. To him it was another day in paradise. This was not the only such misadventure with Chidera and Somto. I remember on another occasion, I had signed up for Mary Kay with my limited resources. I came back home one day and Somto had pulled out all the makeup and ruined them. That was the end of my Mary Kay career.

Day in, day out, we repeated the routine as I realized I was not alone, I had my first son who was very resourceful. From sending him to fetch diaper and milk bottle, to asking him to hold his baby brother while I took a shower or cooked for the family, I realized I was not completely alone as I groomed my son Chidera to be my big helper. Chidera was just four when Ikechi was born, but like his father he was natural at taking care of babies. I got him to sit still and hold his brother while watching television; I told him the importance of supporting the baby's floppy fragile head. I also showed him the right position to hold a baby after a feed so he was guaranteed to burp. He also knew how to lay a baby down to sleep as well as how to put him in the baby swing. I remember being in the kitchen most times and Chidera would walk in with a milk bottle and ask me if the bottle was fresh. If I said yes, he would proceed to feed his baby. Chidera knew how to take care of a baby better than most adults.

I remember, watching him get up on his own volition one day to adjust the baby's head while the baby was taking a nap on the baby swing. I fought back tears and thanked God that we had raised a good son. Remembering the help this young man offered at that time, made me thank God daily.

Now that home was organized and functioning with three sons. Tony was doing very well at work. It was at the time when everyone was worried about the approaching year 2000 (Y2K). Anyone with decent computer skills was in high demand. So Tony was on this contract that had him travel to all the fifty states updating computer systems, many times he left early Monday and returned late evening. Things were really looking up. Once again, I attempted to get back into the work force. I called up a couple of legal staffing agencies and each time they would be excited about my qualifications, but they would later inform me that I was over-qualified.

The only option to getting back into the legal profession was to take the bar exam and be licensed to practice law in any state of my choice or have a complete career change. Even when I insisted I did not mind a paralegal job with my law degree, they refused to give me the jobs, they felt that if they offered a lawyer a paralegal job, it would be beneath them.

Finally, I decided to get some computer training so that I could improve my chances of getting a computer job. We had all the boys in day care and I went to school. I had just finished this school and was gearing up to start applying for jobs with my new qualifications when the unthinkable happened.

Guess what? I was pregnant again.

While we lived in the roach infested town home, Maureen had come to visit one day and brought her friend who just migrated to the United States. Her name was Angela. Maureen had previously told me a lot about Angela and she said she thought we would get along fine. Angela was married to Kunle, who later became friends with Tony, we got along really well and most days she would make the long drive from Carrollton to Richardson to come visit so that her son Simi and the boys could play. Sometimes we would go shopping at Walmart and talk about all the things we would buy when we had money. We would load all the boys in the back seat. We really had our hands full. Sometimes we looked crazy running around with that many children between us. Sometimes older women stopped us in the stores, especially me with a limp, juggling three children and carrying one they could not see yet, they would just smile and say, "You got your hands full."

Truly, I say it takes a certain level of insanity to have these many children in the United States, I do not know what we were thinking. One thing is this, when I was not out with Angela doing grocery shopping or window shopping because we could not afford much then, I was sitting at home building my strength and my relationship with God. I am sure Angela will have a good laugh reading this. It has been a long journey to discovery.

20

THANKING GOD FOR EVERYTHING

Discovering I was pregnant with Kelechi was different, I had come of age, I was more aware of who I was and my circumstances. My loneliness had deepened in some ways, but eased off a bit with my friendship with Angela. We were two different people though, she was more of less a social being who liked to make friends and attend functions. I was a charismatic being who felt more at home alone. She would convince me to go out with her, at times I would honor her invitation to go out and while I was there I wanted to retreat back to my safety nest. I needed to have time alone to reason this huge responsibility out.

Somehow a lot was happening on the inside, there was this day that I needed to buy diapers for the boys. I had three sons and one on the way. When I needed to go to the grocery stores in the past, I would get the three boys ready, wait in front of my complex with them and there was bound to be someone who would offer us a ride to the grocery store across the road, remember I had refused to drive and Tony was on the Y2K project. So this day, I had the two older boys in tow behind me and clutching Ikechi in my unique cerebral palsy Mama clutch. This made any one watching uncomfortable that I was going to drop him, it was an awkward grip, but one that never dropped a baby before. My friend Gina who you will meet soon said that grip reminded her of how an animal grips her young by the neck while going on all fours. Anyway we went in our usual pattern to seek out a ride to the grocery stores.

We waited and waited and no one offered us a ride. I heard the Holy Spirit say to me, "Go home and change and by the time you come out, I will have a ride waiting to take you." I was not sure I heard right as I examined the dress that I was wearing. It was a matronly looking dress and I did not see any reason for the Lord to ask me to change the dress, in fact this is the type of dress that I felt will make the Lord mighty proud of me. I waited for a couple more minutes and I heard it again this time loud and clear. I asked my sons to come with me as we headed back to the apartment. I was fuming. I left the boys by the door and rushed up to change. Quickly,

I found another dress, I jumped in it and headed to the door with the boys. Now my apartment was far from the road, it was toward the end of the first row of town homes. As I stepped out of the door and tried to lock it behind me and the boys. A man in his car on the streets, shouted out to me, "Hi ma'am , do you need a ride?" Initially it seemed he was talking to someone else. As he repeated the question, I realized this was the ride that the Lord had promised me. I hurriedly gathered my dons as we made it in to the car. Once we were seated, I was quiet and subdued. 'What do you want from me, Lord?' I inquired as we made it to the grocery store. He let me know that there was nothing wrong with the first dress, he wanted to make sure that I heard his voice and I recognized it and that he wanted me to obey that voice even when it did not make logical sense to me. I was in awe of God.

I have always said that it was that encounter with God that happened in that roach infested apartment that helped me find my way in the wilderness. Everything that happened in that townhome had deep spiritual meaning to me, made me understand things better. He showed me the clear path to my purpose and prepared me for the journey ahead. I think the reason that my time and place was ideal was because I had very few distractions and I was willing to listen, trust, and obey. In my entire life I had not felt the presence of God like I felt it in that place and time. It was not Kelechi's pregnancy that made us leave Richardson, nor was it the roaches, it was a sudden event.

Daddy was doing well traveling all over, we were very comfortable to the point that we had three television sets in one town home, our lease was almost over and we contemplated renewing. One weekend, Tony was home and relaxing from a long week when he heard Chidera playing with some other boys in the complex, something made him look out of the window. As quiet as he was, Chidera in this unrecognizable loud voice was beating his chest and advancing toward another boy and he was asking the boy, "Want a piece of me?" Tony was in shock, he opened the window and asked him to come back home. Later that day, he talked to me with worry in his eyes, and told me it was time to leave here, we did not want to raise a thug. The next weekend Tony and his good friend Carlton started to look for apartments, they were going to find an apartment in Carrollton. It was a better neighborhood to raise children and we would be there till we bought our own home. The idea of moving to Carrollton was a welcomed one, we had a lot of friends living there; Angela could easily make it to my apartment and we could escape to the stores while Tony and the boys slept. Tony found an apartment in Carrollton. He wanted to show me how proud of me he was for running a great home, so when I told him I did not want to take anything from Richardson to Carrollton because of the roaches, he obliged. Once our lease was over, we packed up our personal belongings, making sure there were no roaches, and with the help of Carlton and movers Tony moved us into the apartment before leaving for work that weekend. We did not take a single piece of furniture, he bought everything new, once we got to the new apartment, we made sure the movers kept our belongings on the balcony while we sprayed them with insecticide till we were convinced that the roaches were gone.

Soon I made the apartment beautiful. I was more relaxed, so I was able to show off my decorating skills. Someone once said that if you lived in a home and came to my apartment you would desire to live an apartment. I spent my day cleaning, cooking and raising our sons. Tony in turn was happy and was looking forward to better things. He had plans to take the New York Bar Exams. Every week he gave me my pocket money once he got home. I could use it for whatever I desired. On Angela's end, things were looking up for them too, her husband had a fairly decent job and had just passed his exams to practice as a pharmacist. We stopped shopping at Walmart and graduated to Sac and Save for food and J. C. Penny's and Target for other things. Every night when our families slept we escaped to the stores.

One day, she came to see me and was very excited, she informed me that her husband had passed his exams and that they were ready to enter the league of professionals in America. I was very happy for her. She also told me that they were going to buy a house. Wow!

There was something really encouraging about the progress that these two were making; by this time, they had a second son, Stephen, and had bought new cars. If they could accomplish this much in such a short time, then anybody could. I was so happy for them. I was not envious, understanding the struggles we had been through, I just felt those kind of dreams were too farfetched.

In the meantime, whenever we went out to Target, we would see incredible household items, they were not too expensive and it would be a lot of gain to collect those pieces one at a time and build a collection, after all I was getting fifty dollars a month from Tony. Before then Angela had asked me to go to their builder's design center to help her make the tile and wallpaper choices, our lives were changing, we were now dreaming of things that we would never had imagined a few years back. All the families in our group were moving up.

I was still nursing dreams of having a girl.

In my imagination all my symptoms were different this time, I did not want to find out the sex of the baby. I had gone back to work because I did not want to be idle while pregnant. Every day we dropped the boys at daycare and then Tony dropped me off at Stream International, a company where I did technical support with my newly acquired computer skills. Stream was a good place to work, I had a good manager and he stood up in my favor when irate customers picked on my accent. I would never forget this irate customer that escalated my call to my manager and my manager, having confidence in my work, was trying to convince him to give me a chance to help him.

The customer had said he could not tell if he was speaking to a man or woman, referring to my deep voice, and my manager had the most impressive answer. He said he did not ask the customer to sleep with me so my gender was not important, with that the customer kept quiet as I successfully helped him.

Another very funny incident that happened at Stream was during my pregnancy with Kelechi, I got hungry at lunch time, but I did not like to leave the premises so I decided I was going to bring my own lunch. So this day, the lunch for that day was going to be leftover fish with tomato sauce that I scooped over noodles. At lunch time, pregnant and starving, I went to the refrigerator to retrieve my lunch and then put it in the microwave. I had just started warming this food when I heard people asking who was warning the foul smelling food, being pregnant and with unique taste buds, I had added some cray fish powder and habanero peppers for better taste. I quickly pulled my plastic container out of the microwave tied it in a bag and put it in the trash can under my table. When the security guards went round investigating the source of the foul smell I said nothing to them. That was the last day I took food to work.

One day at work, I fell. Since I was pregnant I needed to go to the emergency room to have the baby checked out. Since this was the fourth pregnancy and knowing my risk of premature birth and the fact that I had been warned of shorter pregnancies as I had more children, I braced myself for the worst. Everything about this pregnancy told me it was different. I had secretly bought a few little girl dresses. I had just settled down to the sonogram when the loud mouthed technician declared she could see the baby's organ and thinking it was my first, she announced it was a boy. I just burst out crying. I knew this was our last baby, Tony had warned me that we were not going to have any more after this and we decided no matter the sex we were going to close this chapter by thanking God. That was why we chose the name Kelechi. His decision was also informed based on the fact that when my father heard that we were expecting again he said, "Chinwe Onye Chineke mere Ihe omere gi, o wu anya Ukwu." For one who has experienced such favor from God asking for more will be greed. Tony told me this was the end of the road with child bearing.

Once the sonogram showed it was a boy, I took just a day to grieve the disappointment of not having a girl, then I encouraged myself by asking myself a couple of questions. Did you believe you could have one? You are one blessed woman. Are you not being ungrateful here? Does God not know what you need?

By the next day I returned the dresses to Target and bought some jeans and t-shirts. Counting my blessings.

In October of that year, surprisingly at forty weeks of gestation, this handsome boy made his entry.

That morning at the hospital. I was not having any contractions, but I knew all I needed to say at the front desk was that I was having contractions. My mother in law had come with me because she said she had heard so much about my labor and she wanted to witness it herself. Lolo has an incredible sense of humor, she had a way with words that made you crack up. As we got to the labor room she said she heard that I shoot the babies out like easy poop. We laughed so hard. When we were in the labor room, the nurses asked who was the pregnant one between us, Lolo was not amused at that.

Before Tony left us that morning, he had given clear instructions, this was what he said: "I am going into the office to inform them that our baby is coming today, I know you, please do not have the baby before I get back."

This time he had a cellphone and a pager, I could reach him directly.

As usual, prep work started and fifteen minutes later Kelechi was here. My mother-in-law was blown away. She was so happy. She called Tony as he just made it to his office. She called to congratulate him on the birth of his new son. He was not happy that he did not witness the delivery, but he was full of gratitude as we thanked God. Kelechi!

Baby Kelechi was a miracle and a sight for sore eyes. A miracle because I never expected to have a pregnancy that would get to forty weeks. He had a lot of hair and had very light skin tone like his grandma and myself.

Bringing Kelechi home and settling back to our routine was a breeze, I was an old hand at these things by this time, everything was going well. Every morning, on his way to work, Tony would drop the boys at the daycare. One day he was running late and called me to find a way to get the boys from the daycare at the end of the day. I left Baby Kelechi at home and rushed to pick them up. When I got there, I met one of the teachers, she did not know the kids had a mom since she hardly saw me. She always saw their dad and wondered what the story was. That was how I met my friend Gina. Gina had four children of her own all in the same age group as mine. I told her about the new baby and she gave us all a ride back to our apartment and came up to meet the baby.

Gina was married to a rich guy. She drove a suburban and driving around with the boys and her own children was a breeze. Gina came to my life at a time when I had zero support from anywhere. Whenever she could, she took the three older boys out with her kids and pleaded with me not to do any house work, but instead to bond with the baby. By the time they returned I would have cleaned and cooked. I was not used to having that much time. Sometimes she scolded me for that because she would let me know that she left her own chores to give me the blessing of time with the baby. We continue to be friends to this day. I appreciated what Gina did for me at that time. It showed me that the Lord would raise help from unexpected quarters for his children. At a time that I thought God was finished with me. He sent me help.

From this time on, everything was stable and calm. I collected everything that the designer Michael Graves had in Target; they were stainless steel periwinkle and red. I was keeping all the boxes at Angela's house and dreaming of having my own house. The Michael Graves collection gave me something to look forward to; I spent every dollar of my pocket money on them, till Kunle stumbled by the boxes of merchandise in his house one day and he asked his wife who owned them and she said they were mine. He wanted to confirm ownership of the items so he invited us to their house. Tony returned later that day with boxes of household goods, wondering the wisdom in having all these things when there was no room to store them in our apartment. Over the years, I have understood a lot about myself. When I am searching for answers, I keep myself occupied. The Michael Graves pieces kept me sane. After his disappointment, my husband created a space for my wares at the outside storage. He did not have to wait too long to uncover the wisdom in my action.

In the meantime, Angela's new house was a huge fascination for me. She spent no time in trying to make it nice, so many times she invited me to help her decorate, she had the means and boldness to do so. She had a yellow accent wall, the furniture was purple leather. She was living the American dream. Looking back at these times, I know she would have a good laugh considering that they live in a house that is ten times bigger than the one they had.

A few months after Kelechi was born, Tony asked me to get in the car. He drove me to this huge house in Allen, Texas. He asked me if I liked it, I said yes, but I did not think much of it; I don't like to raise my hopes unnecessarily. He later informed me this was our new house and it was at the stage where I could pick the upgrades. Every artistic gift I had suppressed in the years of famine resurfaced. I was in my element! Guess what room was the first to be decorated? Yes! The kitchen, with all my Michael Graves pieces! When I was choosing the wallpaper for the kitchen I was not in doubt, I already had a vision. Instantly, I graduated from an unwise woman to a woman of vision. My husband was so proud of me. Decorating the house gave birth to my decorating career. It was at this this stage that I met two more people. The first was Angela, who lived next door to me. We became instant friends, the one thing about my friendship with Angela was that she believed in me and cared deeply about me. She was expecting her daughter, Ainsley. We were stay at home moms and spent our days decorating our homes while bonding over lunch. We are still friends today.

Then there was Sister Priscilla and her husband William, our friendship was an unusual one as we did not have a lot in common, but she did not care. I was an introvert, but most times Sister Priscilla would show up at my door not caring what I thought. I appreciate that she forced that friendship. She is battling cancer at the moment. Please pray for her. Some other friends were Fehintola, Sister Tina, Ify, and Sister Miran. All great friends.

We were finally becoming part of the American dream, still my heart was still back in Nigeria. I really did not feel like I belonged here. It was at this stage that my family decided I needed a change of scenery. I had been through so much in the last six years. There were a lot of achievements to show for the years, yet I was not happy, so my Uncle Sam decided it was time that I went on an all-expense paid trip to Nigeria to decide if I was going to go back home to stay or remain in the United States.

I went on that first trip to Nigeria with none of my sons. I spent time with my sister, Ndidi; it was beautiful, but I missed my family so much. One thing I realized was that I no longer felt like I belonged in Nigeria, I found myself comparing everything with how things were in Dallas and being irritated. Don't get me wrong, staying in my sister's house was like staying in a five-star hotel anywhere in the world. I did not want for anything, the problem was, I was a realist. I knew very well that a rolling stone gathered no moss and that there was no way I would leave the life that God had prepared before me and return to the world I left already.

Everything was strange to me. This was coming from someone that had kept her life in limbo in the past five years, not wanting to make permanent decisions in the land that God had sent me. It was no different from the Israelites who were being taken to the promised land and all they could remember was what they left behind. By the time I was packing up to go home, I was more than ready. My mindset had changed. On my way home, I stopped in London to visit my parents. I looked around in my parents multi-million dollar home and I wondered why my memory of this place was larger than life. Everything seemed smaller than I remembered. One of the things that irritated me was the hardness of the water, also the low water pressure. I was suddenly grateful to God for how far he had brought us, struggles and all. I spent the last days of my trip with my parents, feeling like a little girl again. When the time came to go home, I looked straight ahead, embracing the life ahead of me, ready to conquer. As the plane touched the ground ten hours later, I was in tears. This was the land that the Lord has blessed! I was back with my heart and my every fiber of my being.

The next few years were years of discovery. It was like one discovering life again. I was a new mum and a new wife. I took on a job with Experian that was down the road from my house. Every morning Tony dropped the boys at the day care and dropped me at work before he went to his office. In the evening, he retraced his steps, got me and then the boys. Life was finally falling into a beautiful routine. It was at this point also that we found our way back to Redeemed Christian Church of God.

Several years ago on one of our short rides from my apartment to Angela's house, we had packed the children in the car and we were suddenly involved in a car accident. In the accident, I hit my knee on the dashboard. It left my knee badly battered, I was in a lot of pain. The knee had very little cushioning and I took arthritis medication daily to cope. The doctors suggested a couple of surgeries; the first surgery was a tendon repair. It was at this time that I realized there was no little surgery. Each time there would be months of physical therapy then there would be pain and muscle weakness. The unpleasant thing about surgery to repair is that your hope is to relieve pain, but it will give you more pain before giving relief; unlike reconstructive surgery where you have pain, but you have hope of improvement. That surgery was my first after a long period of grace from the surgeries in London. My only hope here was to relieve pain. Before I could see any sign of relief, I went through tremendous pain. This was when Tony went to New York to take his bar exams, he had asked me if he should delay his trip. I said no because we needed to get this bar exam done and focus on better life, he was away for two months, by the time he came back he met a skinnier new bride. I went through the initial pain and then emerged better. That was a simple surgery, but a few months later the pain returned while I worked with Experian and I had to leave work to have another surgery to alleviate the pain. This was the pain that challenged me the most, apart from the fact that my recovery took six months even when the the doctor told me would take two weeks. I was on a walker that I could not lose. I forgot how to walk, I was completely immobile and gained so much weight, fear gripped me. I was certain I had made the greatest mistake of my adult life by desiring a pain free life. The doctor blamed my complications on cerebral palsy. That was the period I wrote about in my first book that Tony had "the talk" with me. He told me that he knew I had some sort of physical disability when he married me and that he was okay with that, but that he did not see how we could cope with my not walking and four children. It was painful to hear, but that also explains the honesty with which we discussed these issues. He hid the walker and I had to learn how to walk with all the pain and weakness.

The strength came back with the forced physical challenges, but the pain remained off and on through the years for over ten years.

21

PAIN CAN BE GOOD FOR YOU

I do not know about people with other types of physical disability, but living with cerebral palsy you have to learn how to live with constant pain, some of them are occasional due to injury or environmental changes. You learn how to live with it constantly. One of my sons complained of pain at a particular time, they ran all the tests and nothing was wrong. I had a talk with him and I said to him, "Son, if I paid attention to every pain and ache I feel as I open my eyes in the morning, I would not make that first trip to the bathroom." I truly mean it; the mornings are the toughest times. Every muscle aches as I wake up, but daily I resolve to give my best effort. Best effort is truly what life is about. I have a pretty bedside commode by my bed for the days that best effort may not be enough. Thankfully, apart from surgery times, I have never seen a day that the grace of God and best effort did not win.

I find it strange that in my almost fifty years, I am experiencing the least pain. This pain relief came with a whole lot of pain, more than the other times, but the relief has been well worth it. The lessons and benefit from the experiences are priceless too.

Like I said, I had pain off and on through the years, till 2013. Before then I had zero support in my knees and I fell like a pack of cards, the angel in my life at the time was my longtime friend, Ola. Ola and I have known each other since Federal Owerri, which was our secondary school, but we were not very close friends, fast forward several years later we met again at our children's school and since then have built a strong friendship. I am blessed to have a friend like Ola. We are sort of opposites. Ola is a listener; I am a talker. Because she listens, I could try to talk to her about things that are difficult to talk to anybody about and she would get it. Another way we are different is that she is sensitive and I am hardly emotional; I don't know how to show emotions because for a person living with disability emotions, could be misunderstood as another form of challenge.

Because Ola understood me, she had come to understand never to offer unsolicited help. Sometimes it really shattered her kind heart when she could not offer the help and something goes wrong. So this period that my knee was giving me a lot of problems, we had planned to go to the movies, just girls' night out. She came to get me, we both dressed up. I was wearing a short floral dress, we got to the movies and without notice, I went tumbling like Humpty Dumpty. Ola was getting popcorn and turned around and sees me, short dress up, lacy panties in the air. It took a lot of queen's men to get me up. Ola was in tears, she asked what I wanted to do after that, if we should go home? I did not want to mess up the evening. I told her we should still watch the movie. That particular fall was not pretty; I kept a straight face to make Ola feel better, but I was shattered. After that fall, I had a few more. I was now very concerned. I was getting older, I was also heavier.

I could see that my days of mobility were grinding to a halt, I was afraid to leave the safety of my home, yet I did not admit to my friends and family that I was in trouble. I did not want them to worry.

One day, I was talking to my Sister Ihuoma and in the process, I sort of mentioned that my legs were bothering me. She said that I may be surprised what medical science may offer me now. I had my doubts, but I had no choice. I needed to seek help and fast. There was yet another issue, because of the way I dragged my right foot, there was a lot of friction, this made me get a callous on my big toe. Because of that, I decided to find a podiatrist within my insurance network. I found one and went to consult with her. She examined me and took some x-rays, she was shocked. She was screaming. She said it was not medically possible for me to walk on my right foot, that every bone in the foot was misplaced. I truly did not understand what she meant, after the consultation, she said she may be able to get the foot work better, but to do that she needed an orthopedic doctor to help straighten the knee and loosen the very tight hamstrings, if not, it just would not work. Just hearing someone tell me there was more they could offer me at forty-seven years old was like music to my ears. I had so many emotions coming to the surface again. I could not contain myself. On the day of the appointment with the orthopedic surgeon, I could not sleep. I was wondering what they may offer. I was wondering how much my life might change and if this was possible. The doctor got some x-rays of the knee and examined them. He said he could do what the podiatrist wanted, but that he was not the best person to do the job, he said he was going to refer me to another doctor who is an expert in cerebral palsy. I was disappointed, but I took the referral and left.

A few days later. I placed a call to the doctor. His name was Dr. Hukenuik. He was very friendly and related very well with his patients. He was a nerd when it came to fixing bones, muscles, tendon, and nerves. He examined me and tried to decode me and my peculiar body. Initially, he did not offer much promise. He needed different x-rays. Once I got the x-rays he examined them and recognized some issues. By my third visit, I asked him why my body was not even. He asked me to lie down and he measured each part of the leg. To his surprise there was great disparity. He said he would like to fit me with a customized orthotic to see if that would make a difference I wore that for about three months and when I returned he concluded the difference in length was part of the problem, He now told me his treatment plan. He said he could shorten the leg, work on the knees and also the foot at the same time. I asked him if I would look and walk better, he said yes. I could not believe my ears. What? Was this really happening to me. Could it be true? How much better? Thoughts just danced around my head. The same kind of hopeful thoughts I had when the American evangelist said I was healed at the crusade.

The problem was convincing my husband. He eventually agreed. On the day of the surgery we got to the hospital very early, once we were settled, he took a before video. We were expectant, something was about to change. If you understand the way I function, I never look at my leg in the mirror or video because I choose not to.

On that day I intentionally chose to see. I was willing to see it because it was about to change. What I saw shocked me. I was clutching at every piece of furniture in the room to stabilize myself. It was also a jerking movement that explained to me why the boys in my class in the university gave me the nickname "Earthquake." I turned to Tony and asked him if my leg was truly as bad as the video I just saw and he asked me if I did not know that. I said I did not. That day I truly had newfound respect for my husband, I did not know how he summoned up the courage to spend his life with someone that walked that way.

Soon it was time to be wheeled into the theatre, he kissed me as they took me away. I replaced the sad thoughts of the video I just watched with happy thoughts of what I was expecting and what I was going to wake up to.

Chichi, I heard a nurse call me as I came out of anesthesia. I was in a lot of pain, my leg was very heavy. I was shivering and a bit confused. I could recognize my husband by my side; he was worried and puzzled. Puzzled because he just could not imagine how I make my decisions and just go, not considering the risks involved. I knew he may not have approved of the surgery because he liked to think things through. I think it is the project manager in him. Our son Somto had been my accomplice on this journey, he liked the excitement that the treatment plans gave me, but neither Somto nor Tony thought I would actually go through with it at forty-seven . They thought I would lose interest eventually.

No one could understand why I needed this surgery, apart from the fall. I am a believer of the saying, "Nothing ventured, nothing gained." If I did not do this surgery now, I may regret it later and it may be too late.

Tony was happy to see me come out of anesthesia. Now that I was safe, he could call our sons and tell them I just had the surgery and I was okay. I know they had their expectations too.

The next morning, the physical therapist showed up very early. She told me I had to get up and walk around. I could not even imagine sitting up on the bed. I had a cast from the hip to the ankle and everywhere was throbbing with excruciating pain. With her encouragement, I was able to use the walker to make it to the door. They said that I did not have to overdo it. Every time I was alone, my heart would do drumbeats in anticipation of the miracle that was about to unfold. I would look down at the leg in the cast. It lay flat against the hard hospital bed. This was new to me, usually when I laid down before the surgery my knee would jolt up because of the excess length. Now I could see it was flat. There were changes already!

Hope renewed, dream mode activated again. Soon the doctor came in to chat with me, he said everything went well. I could go home the next day, but had come back and see him in the office in two days to take out the stitches and remove cast. Daily, there was a new song on my lips; my life was about to change.

On getting home, everything was difficult, the pain was from every part of my leg, but I was still hopeful.

The pain would not last forever. I had to use a walker. Doctor Humenuik had said that it would take a minimum of six months for recovery. I thought to myself, six months' recovery? Dr. Humenuik did not know me. To my shock, by six months I was still struggling to wean myself of the walker and graduate to the cane, this was with regular therapy. There was weakness and pain. There were days I regretted the surgery. I guess anyone living with disabilities will feel the same way after surgery. We usually know that the recovery will take time and nothing is guaranteed, but each time we go through it we expect faster results.

I had some incredible therapists, I formed great relationships with all of them. One thing they will all tell you is that I was always ready to try anything and that I never quit or got tired. The desire to get better was always so strong in me that I was always willing to try.

I bless the day that I was introduced to Dr. Humenuik; just when I was running out of steam, God sent help through him.

There are several things that would have happened if I did not go through with the surgery. My arthritis would have gotten worse, my back would have packed up, and the foot would have deteriorated. However, from pain that would not go away, it became a blessing in disguise and I cannot believe the pain free life I have now.

Before the surgery, the doctor had looked at me and said I used so much energy to do the most basic things, about three times more energy than others. He said he wanted to give me the chance to do more with less energy. How prophetic is that? It has been a long road to recovery, but it has been worth every pain. God truly works in mysterious ways. Dr. Humenuik also knew how much I liked to dress up and he told me that after recovery I could wear up to three inch heels as long as they were wedge or block.

Talking about the heels bring tears to my eyes. I have always felt sad for not being able to wear regular shoes. Shoes were always a huge issue for me, even if they were good quality, flat and with straps, once I put my foot in them, they disfigure and tilt to one side. Then there were the holes! All my shoes had holes from my leg dragging on the ground. Talking about shoes reminds me of my very own leather mules with an inch heel. This real pretty red pair was bought by my Sister Dora who was living in London at the time, I must have been about four then. When the shoes arrived, I was so excited thinking, "this will be my chance to wear high heel like other girls," but I could not walk in them. Mama put them in her room so I would not wear them because they were not the best kind of shoes for me. Whenever Mama went out I would try them on. One day I found out I could wear them.

Today several dreams that I was too afraid to dream or voice have materialized. Who would have thought that I would wear three inch heels? I wear them with so much ease now.

Journey So Far!

What a journey! What a life! It is few days to my fiftieth birthday. There is no doubt in my mind that the Lord loves me so much. I am blessed beyond measure; words cannot express the gratitude that I have.

"Bless the Lord, O my soul, and forget not all his benefits, who forgives all your iniquity, who heals all your diseases, who redeems your life from the pit, who crowns you with steadfast love and mercy, who satisfies you with good so that your youth is renewed like the eagle's."

(Psalm 103:2-5)

I have been blessed with the ability to dream big, this dream I could not dream, I could not have asked the Lord for this much. This would have been way too much to ask.

Ten years ago when I turned forty I said if God decided to call me home then it would still be a great life. Who would have thought that I would approach fifty in this way? Everything came together in this beautiful way that even the greatest writer could not have imagined, step by step he brought everything together. Every experience, positive and negative, every tear, every disappointment, every rejection, every discrimination, and every tribulation he used as a teaching process for growth. I have come to some understanding as I reach this golden milestone that I am not the driver here. He is in full control. I just need to trust and watch.

Fifty is a place of rest for me, it is a place that I can sit and catch my breath from a journey that has left me breathless. He renews my soul! I have spent so much time begging and pleading to be considered capable. I have tried to prove that what you see on the outside does not determine what I can do or be. Finally, I get to a place of rest, nothing left to prove, nothing left unsaid and undone.

It took a lot of growing up to get here, it took finding comfort and realizing that life really is a lonely journey and that being lonely is not a bad thing, but an opportunity to invite the Holy Spirit. Through this journey I discovered that a desolate place is a blessing.

I cannot end this book if I do not pay a special tribute to the man that God has used to make this life possible. The love of my life, I call him Di m. You are one in a million. I still ask, what in the name of God were you thinking?

In writing this book, it took challenging everything that I hold sacred, it took digging really deeply in personal places to find forgiveness for others and myself. Through this experience, I have found tremendous cleansing and healing. My prayer is that these experiences that helped get me here, will help heal you in any part of your life that is challenged.

My belief is that we can live challenged lives to the fullest if we trust God. This is not end of my story. If you notice, I have intentionally left out stories or experiences that happened in the past ten years other than the surgery. The process of healing continues.

That wound is still very raw and continues to play out.

Right now I am in transit and the next time I get to a stop I will tell some more, I hope you enjoyed reading these stories; writing and reading them was therapeutic for me.

The stories gave me the chance to celebrate the excellent friends and family I have been blessed to have.

If your name was not mentioned here, it will be mentioned at the next stop.

My story continues. Keep reading…

Challenge that which challenges you, do not bury your head in hopelessness and give up without trying.

My Greatest Lesson!

After the reconstructive surgery, I found myself down the path that I was on several years ago when I was a little girl and Mama took me to that crusade. Because I do not ordinarily know that I have a disability, I had to learn to separate fantasy from reality when a change happens.

My expectation was that the surgery would not just make me better, but make me look like everybody else and yes I still nursed that hope. There was a little problem when I recovered fully. The problem was that people still stared at me, initially I pretended not to notice, but in my very open approach, I decided to inquire about that. The next time I saw my friend Ola, I asked her if I could talk to her and she said yes. I told her I wanted her to be really honest with me, I then asked the question, fearing the worst. I asked if my leg was better. She took time and weighed her answer, I could see sadness in her eyes as she gave me her answer. She then said, "If someone does not know you, they will think it was not improved, but for someone that knows you as well as I do, I see the improvements, but I expected much more."

Those were not the answers I was expecting, but I could handle that. I was disappointed to learn it was not perfect, knowing that this was my last shot at perfection.

Some days later, the Lord asked me a question. "If you succeed at this quest for perfection, who will you now become and what will then be your purpose?" He also informed me that my challenges are the reason that he chose me. "My grace will always give you strength. If you are perfect now, who will you then be? The artist formerly known as Chichi?" This put things in perspective for me. I finally get it, I created this way to fulfill a purpose.

> "And we know that in all things God works for the good of those
> who love him, who have been called according to his purpose."
>
> Romans 8:28

All things have worked for good and I am grateful.

TIPS FOR YOUR JOURNEY:

Thank you for journeying with me, I have enjoyed telling these stories, I used real names because I wanted to celebrate all the great people that God has used to teach me.

1) CHOOSE HOW TO SCRIPT YOUR STORY

If you must tell a story, make a resolution how you want it told. It is your story and you can tell it any way you want to, but no one wants to read a vindictive story. Take a moment to think it over and you will find a kinder way to tell the story and give someone the gift of forgiveness. What do you think I would have achieved if I called my mum a wicked name for pushing me? I would continue to hold myself hostage with the actions of a dead person.

2) LAUGH AT YOUR EXPERIENCES

You can find humor in every experience. Even if it was humiliating when it happened, choose to laugh at the awkwardness. Let me give you an example, when I had that fall; It was embarrassing, but telling it now, it is quite funny. Some of these experiences were not very pleasant when they were happening, but I choose how to tell them and in putting humor, I saved my dignity and defused the situation with laughter. The way I described the panties and legs in the air made me feel better, it is bound to make someone else laugh and probably want to share their story that has been haunting them. They will feel they found someone that can relate to their experiences.

3) WHAT IS THE MORAL OF YOUR STORY?

Every story has a moral, if there is no moral to your story then it may not really be worth telling. It may be like a very dry joke, out of taste, and devoid of reason.

Is it necessary? Will sharing it diminish another? If your answer is yes, then save the story till you heal.

4) BE DARING AS YOU JOURNEY

Good things come to those who dare! If you do not try, you can never tell if you would have accomplished something great. We have to be willing to take risks in life. Remember my story about the dance at the party? I tried and it worked in my interest.

5) DREAMS COME TRUE!

I cannot say it enough, dream, dream, and dream. Your dreams can become your reality. It is your greatest life tool. I dream all the time. I am the script writer and the producer of my life movie, the Lord gives me the grace to put it together.

6) ESTEEM YOURSELF

There is a reason that the word is self-esteem, it is your God-given right. It is your power to speak all things good to yourself. No one owes you that. If you do not get the affirmation from any other person, it will not bother you.

7) BE VULNERABLE

Freedom comes from being vulnerable.

Why hold unto negative experiences like you want to have a franchise on it. Life is a gift. Negative things always happen. They are not meant to destroy us but to build, several of these stories made me who I am today. Like a quilt, each piece came together to weave this story. I proudly own my stories. Do you own yours?

8) EMBRACE YOUR UNIQUENESS

Every part of my body including the crooked leg make me who I am today. I am unique, beautiful, and mysterious. There can never be another Chichi Iro. The sculptor equipped me for all he knew I would be needing for the journey. I understand my purpose and how it turns into what I am supposed to be doing while I am here. I am an encourager. My bad leg makes people feel I can relate to them.

9) CELEBRATE ALL THINGS GOOD

If you are an advocate of good, good will follow you. You sow what you reap, remember the parable of the sower. Sow good. Good will return to you.

10) LOVE IS THE GREATEST

Be a lover, give love freely, and receive love with open arms.

First accept the love of God. No matter your circumstances, the Lord loves you.

Love others. Give others the gift of love even if they do not deserve it.

Accept love. Most people repel love, they do not believe in themselves so they do not believe they can be loved by another. Receive love with open arms.

Finally believe in yourself and your abilities. You can do this!

Live life to the fullest.

Keep hope alive.

Be Enabled!

Chichi Iro.

Manufactured by Amazon.ca
Bolton, ON